THE INCREDIBLE POWER OF
KINGDOM
AUTHORITY

THE INCREDIBLE POWER OF
KINGDOM

GETTING AN UPPER HAND ON THE UNDERWORLD

AUTHORITY

ADRIAN ROGERS

BROADMAN
&HOLMAN
PUBLISHERS

NASHVILLE, TENNESSEE

0–8054–1676–5

Published by Broadman & Holman Publishers
Nashville, Tennessee

Dewey Decimal Classification: 248
Subject Heading: CHRISTIAN LIVING

Unless otherwise noted, Scripture quotations are from the King James Version. Quotations identified NKJV are from the New King James Version, copyright © 1979, 1980, 1982, Thomas Nelson, Inc., Publishers. Quotations identified NIV are from the Holy Bible, New International Version, copyright © 1973, 1978, 1984 by International Bible Society. All uses of italic in biblical text has been added by the author for emphasis.

1 2 3 4 5 6 7 8 9 10 07 06 05 04 03 02

CONTENTS

PREFACE

Desraeli said, "The author who speaks about his own books is almost as bad as a mother who speaks about her own children."

That is a bit intimidating to me for two reasons. First, I wrote this book, and second, I gave birth to it; and now I am going to talk about it.

In a sense this book was more "born" than written. I was impregnated with the idea of Kingdom Authority about forty years ago. Most things born don't gestate for forty years. Yet little by little this volume grew inside the womb of my mind until it saw the light of day.

And there were labor pains. I have written other books with comparative ease, but not this one. I don't mean to imply that this is a theological or literary masterpiece. It is neither. I believe, however, that Satan opposed the writing of *The Incredible Power of Kingdom Authority*.

There were interruptions, sidetracks, emergencies, and even trivial matters that worked to abort this book.

One day I dropped to my knees and claimed the very victory that I was writing about. Yes, I had prayed before, but this prayer was one of desperate boldness. From then on, the labor pains subsided and the book was born.

I have good news and better news. The good news is that we can be heaven born and heaven bound. The better news is that along with that comes Kingdom Authority, if we will only exercise it. There is no greater desire that I have for my life, the lives of my family members, and for you, dear reader, than that you might discover the truth and experience the vitality of Kingdom Authority.

ACKNOWLEDGEMENTS

It would be monumental arrogance for me to fail to give thanks to those who have assisted me in writing this book.

I first learned the principles of spiritual authority from Watchman Nee's book Spiritual Authority. Then these truths were reinforced as I listened to Bill Gothard in the early 1970s teach about true biblical submission. Also, Major Ian Thomas spoke volumes to my heart in his classic work The Saving Life of Christ.

I also wish to express profound gratitude to my editor, Leonard Goss, and to the staff at Broadman & Holman for their guidance to me and their incredible patience with me in waiting for what turned out to be a long overdue book. May God show them the mercy that they have shown to me.

Next, I give a big thank you to Julia Flanagan and the staff at Love Worth Finding Ministries. Julia is a gifted writer in her own right and was much help in transcription and editorial work.

Also, I remember my administrative assistant, Linda Glance, for helping in so many ways—big and small.

Also, I give thanks to my precious daughter, Gayle, who gave me the idea for the subtitle of this book: Getting an Upper Hand on the Underworld.

And last of all to my dear wife, Joyce, from whose writings I have quoted freely and who has put into practice, as well as anyone that I know, the principles of kingdom authority. I am blessed beyond measure by her life.

To Jesus be the Glory!

GETTING AN UPPER HAND ON THE UNDERWORLD

When you were born again, you *were born to win!* With your new birth came Kingdom Authority that fitted you for victory. Kingdom Authority is the God-given mandate of Christians to exercise control over the world in the name of Jesus and under His oversight. The Bible says, "For whatsoever is born of God overcometh the world: and this is the victory that overcometh the world, even our faith. Who is he that overcometh the world, but he that believeth that Jesus is the Son of God?" (1 John 5:4–5). Do you believe in Jesus Christ? Then you should be living in victory.

We are born to win, not born to lose. This is life-changing, liberating truth, so why don't we experience victory all the time? Circumstances arise that discourage. People say things that cause us to feel defeated. We find ourselves fighting a losing battle against unholy desires. Why are we fighting a battle already lost when we could enjoy a victory already won?

SATAN'S UNDERWORLD

There is a ruthless, cruel underworld system that wars against our welfare, happiness, and joy. The Mafia and crime bosses of this world are amateurs compared to this syndicate, ruled by the prince of darkness and the master of deception who wears many disguises and has many aliases. "And no marvel; for Satan himself is transformed into an angel of light" (2 Cor. 11:14).

No matter what face he wears, Satan has one overmastering ambition, one burning desire—to dethrone the Almighty and to place himself upon the highest throne of the universe. Isaiah 14 describes Satan's fall in this way:

> How you have fallen from heaven,
>   O morning star, son of the dawn!
> You have been cast down to the earth,
>   you who once laid low the nations!
> You said in your heart,
>   "I will ascend to heaven;
> I will raise my throne
>   above the stars of God;
> I will sit enthroned on the mount of assembly,
>   on the utmost heights of the sacred mountain.
> I will ascend above the tops of the clouds;
>   I will make myself like the Most High."
> But you are brought down to the grave,
>   to the depths of the pit.
>
> —Isaiah 14:12–15 NIV

At one time the devil served in heaven as a mighty angel, but he rebelled against God. And when he fell, a third of the angels fell with him and became disembodied spirits. We call them demons today. The devil is now the lord of these fallen angels, and together they form a demonized, organized, and mobilized power of satanic wickedness. Paul reminds us, "For we wrestle not against flesh and blood, but against principalities, against powers, against the rulers of the darkness of this world, against spiritual wickedness in high places" (Eph. 6:12).

We may think our enemy is flesh and blood. But the true enemy is not the government or the Republicans or the Democrats, your wife or your wife's family, or your boss. And this may come as a shock, but your enemy is not the pornographer, the liquor baron, or the drug pusher. They are only victims of our common enemy. The reason that so many times we don't win the battle is that *we never show up for the war!* We are not wrestling against flesh and blood! The enemy is a spiritual foe, and the battle is a spiritual battle.

Why is Satan's hatred so intense against mankind? Because he tried once to overthrow the King, but failed (see Matt. 4:1–11). He knows he cannot defeat Jesus. So he tries to cripple those whom God loves. It's the same tactic the underworld mob uses when it tries to coerce enemies by threatening their children. This is nothing new. Evil men and women have always known that the way to hurt someone is to hurt someone else whom he loves.

Be warned! From Satan's viewpoint you are a pawn in his game of cosmic chess. Plans have already been made in Satan's underworld to sabotage you, your loved ones, and your family. How does he plan to gain the upper hand over you? He uses two chief weapons—the world and the flesh. Together, with his orchestration, they make up a trinity of evil—the *world*, the *flesh*, and the *devil*. They are interactive forces in a three-pronged attack.

THE WORLD IS THE EXTERNAL FOE

"Love not the world, neither the things that are in the world. If any man love the world, the love of the Father is not in him. For all that is in the world, the lust of the flesh, and the lust of the eyes, and the pride of life, is not of the Father, but is of the world" (1 John 2:15–16). In this context, the "world" is not referring to the world of *people*. God loves that world (John 3:16). Neither is it the world of *nature*. This is God's handiwork, and he has declared it good (Gen. 1:31). The winsome nature of God is seen in the beauty of his creation. The earth and the heavens are full of his glory! To love God is to love his created world.

Heav'n above is softer blue.
Earth around is sweeter green!
Something lives in every hue
Christless eyes have never seen:
Birds with gladder songs o'erflow,
Flowers with deeper beauties shine,
Since I know as now I know,
I am His, and He is mine.

—George W. Robinson

To understand what our passage in 1 John means by the "world," let's look at the original Greek which is *kosmos,* meaning an "orderly arrangement" or "system." In this context, the world that we should *not* love is an ungodly system masterminded by Satan himself. The unwavering purpose of this "world" is to take you from God by squeezing you, molding you, and conforming you into an ungodly and destructive lifestyle.

On the surface, this lifestyle may seem alluring, pleasant, and even helpful and beautiful. Most people (and sadly many Christians) are swept away by it. It's certainly not always the hideous way of life we expect from Satan's handiwork. But it's the same system that Adam struggled against. It is the same bad eggs re-scrambled. It's not a new world order; it's just the same old world order. Other words for the world's system might be "conventional wisdom" or "political correctness" or "the good life."

Everything in this world system is warped by sin. It is a mind-set of people without God and his Word, and it exerts tremendous pressure on our lives. We see the major components of this system in 1 John 2:15–16:

- **Sensual Pleasures.** "The lust of the flesh." This would include inordinate desires in the areas of food, drugs, sex, alcohol, laziness, violence, amusement, etc. (see Gal. 5:16–21).
- **Selfish Possessions.** "The lust of the eyes." This speaks of the desire to have more and more of everything that entices the eyes. The stomach is not the only thing that has an appetite. Eyes enamored by the world have an insatiable appetite. A wise philosopher once said, "To whom little is not enough, nothing is enough" (see Gen. 3:1–7).
- **Stubborn Pride.** "The pride of life." This is the desire for importance. A desire to lord yourself over others—to be self-sufficient, the best, and the greatest. It was pride that turned an angel into the devil. It is pride that escorts the human peacock as he struts into hell. And it is pride that has ruined the human race and turned this world into a graveyard (see James 4:16).

THE FLESH IS THE INTERNAL FOE

We must also come to grips with an enemy inside ourselves that the Scripture calls the flesh. The description of the flesh is not a pretty picture: "Now the works of the flesh are manifest, which are these; Adultery, fornication, uncleanness, lasciviousness, idolatry, witchcraft, hatred, variance, emulations, wrath, strife, seditions, heresies, envyings, murders, drunkenness, revellings, and such like: of the which I tell you before, as I have also told you in time past, that they which do such things shall not inherit the kingdom of God" (Gal. 5:19–21).

The *flesh,* as the word is used here, is not your flesh and bones, hide and hair, nerves and sinews. Many of us may be carrying some extra pounds of that kind of flesh, but it is not the "flesh" that is spoken of here.

This *flesh* is an inherited predisposition to do evil. Our English word comes from the Greek word *sarx,* which speaks of our "human" or "carnal" nature. We received it from our parents, but it roots all the way back to Adam. As someone once said, we all have "fated genes." The flesh is like software programming the hardware of our brain and body. And it has a virus called sin.

It may surprise you to know that you don't need the devil in order to sin. I read of a youngster who hit his sister, called her a bad name, and spit on her. His mother said, "John, the devil made you do that." He replied, "The devil made me hit her and call her a bad name, but spitting on her was my idea." We would have a rude awakening if we had the omniscient eyes of God to see just how much of our sin is an inside job for which *we* can take the credit—or should we say the blame? (see James 4:1).

You might as well admit it—you have an internal foe within the gates of your personality called the flesh. You are a sinner by nature and if Satan didn't exist, you would go on sinning without his help. He does exist, however, and he uses the world and the flesh in his battle against mankind.

SATAN IS THE INFERNAL FOE

The mastermind who orchestrates this whole conspiracy is Satan himself. He is the dark prince. Jesus called him "the prince of this world" (John 14:30). The apostle Paul called him "the god of this world" (2 Cor. 4:4).

Satan is a consummate liar, and he is spiritually wicked, brilliantly stupid, and hideously beautiful. He wants to pull the veil of darkness over his activities. For a while he may persuade sophisticates that he does not exist at all. They think of him as a mythological character or in the comic sense as a little guy in a red suit with a pitchfork trying to catch somebody bending over.

If he can't convince people that he doesn't exist, then he tries another route—spreading the lie that the devil is *only* in hell and that is where he reigns. The truth is that he is not in hell. He will be in hell one day. When he goes to hell, he will be incarcerated and tormented there. He will not reign there. Hell was prepared for the devil and his angels, but he is not there yet!

Satan comes against you to obsess, depress, and defeat. Many have fallen and are overtly worshiping Satan in the most gross, blasphemous, and obscene ways. And still others are covertly worshiping him in the dark, hidden recesses of life where people think they will never be found out! Others follow him unwittingly as an "angel of light."

Let me give you some of the names and descriptions that have been given to him in the Bible. He is called the deceiver. He is called a liar. He is called a murderer. He is called the accuser of the brethren, the tempter, the prince of the power of the air, the destroyer, the evil one. Like many in the underworld, he has his aliases.

The world, the flesh, and the devil have struck an unholy alliance for your humiliating defeat and destruction. Think of your flesh as a pool of gasoline. Think of the world system as a lighted match. Think of Satan as the one who has struck the match and flings it at you. The searing flames that leap up to consume and destroy you can be traced to this devilish arsonist!

It Is Time for Some Good News!

The good news is that you have glorious Kingdom Authority over this trinity of evil. First Peter 5:8–10 promises God will make us strong, firm, and steadfast against the ploys of Satan: "Be sober, be vigilant; because your adversary the devil, as a roaring lion, walketh about, seeking whom he may devour: Whom resist stedfast in the faith, knowing that the same afflictions are accomplished in your brethren that are in the world. But the God of all grace, who hath called us unto his eternal glory by Christ Jesus, after that ye have suffered a while, make you perfect, stablish, strengthen, settle you."

- You *can* detect Satan's schemes and overcome his world system.
- You *can* live with victory over the desires of your flesh. Habits, attitudes, desires, worries, and dissipation must yield as you exercise authority over your mind, emotions, and will.
- You *can* actually put Satan and his demons to flight. You don't have be afraid of him—*he will be afraid of you!*

Satan wants you to close this book NOW! He feels you have already read too much. He wants to keep you defeated. And the way to do that is to keep you in the dark.

Even now your own mind may tell you there is little hope for you. You may be like the cat who had his tail stepped on so many times that when anyone came into the room, he would simply turn around, stick out his tail, and wait for it to be stepped on. Like this cat you may have programmed yourself for defeat. You're headed straight for a self-fulfilling prophecy. You think you'll lose . . . and regrettably so, you often do!

Perhaps the best you hope for is merely survival. I heard of a football coach who sent out a former player to recruit players for the team. The recruiter asked, "What kind of a player do we want, coach?"

The coach responded, "Well, you know the man who gets knocked down and stays down? We don't want him. Then there is the guy who gets up when he is knocked down; but when he is knocked down again, he stays down. We don't want him either. But there is the guy who keeps getting up no matter how many times he gets knocked down."

The recruiter said, "That's the guy we want, isn't it, coach?"

"No!" the coach bellowed. "I want you to find the guy who is knocking everybody down. *That's* the guy I want!"

How about you? Wouldn't you like to be on offense in the spiritual realm for a change? Wouldn't you rather get the upper hand on the underworld and discover Kingdom Authority? Thank God you can get up when you are knocked down, but there is more!

Sometimes a Christian may boast, "I am not afraid of the devil." Well, that is all well and good, and Jesus has taught us that we are not to be terrified of our adversaries. The truth of the matter, however, is that if you understand Kingdom Authority, the devil ought to be afraid of you!

Remember that we are in a war, and it is a fight to the finish. There can be no truce and no neutrality. Through the conquest of Calvary we are already in the place of victory. "But thanks be to God, which giveth us the victory through our Lord Jesus Christ" (1 Cor. 15:57).

When Jesus commissioned seventy to go out and preach, he gave his authority along with their marching orders. When they came back, they had the glow of victory written all over their faces: "And the seventy returned again with joy, saying, Lord, even the devils are subject unto us through thy name. And he said unto them, I beheld Satan as lightning fall from heaven. Behold, I give unto you power to tread on serpents and scorpions, and over all the power of the enemy: and nothing shall by any means hurt you" (Luke 10:17–19).

When Jesus said, "I give unto you power to tread on serpents," he used the Greek word *dunamis,* which literally means ability and strength. And when he gave them power over the enemy, he used the Greek word *exousia,* which means the official right or authority to act. They had power, and they had Kingdom Authority.

Exousia focuses on the right to use the power rather than on the power itself. It is a personal right because of position, standing, or by delegation. It may be conferred in legal, political, social, or spiritual realms.

As we go deeper, we will learn that Jesus, in his humanity, received his power from the Holy Spirit and his authority from his intimate relationship with the Father. He now has conferred on us that same power and authority. We can get an upper hand on the underworld.

While Satan has been defeated and rendered ultimately powerless against the Spirit-filled believer, he has not yet surrendered. And he will not give up without a fight. He is going to press on to do whatever damage he can through deception, threats, and intimidation. And this is a part of the plan of God. God's plan for us is *not* immunity from struggle but *victory through struggle.* In this victory we must appropriate what God has already established.

THE AUTHORITY TO CALL THEIR BLUFF!

When our family lived in Florida, we lived near the Indian River, which is a saltwater lagoon that stretches many miles up and down the east coast of Florida. It is a very beautiful body of water that is perfect for sailing. In the evenings, it was my joy to come home, kick off my shoes, put on an old pair of trousers, get one or two of the kids, and go sail into the sunset on this river. What fun we had telling stories, laughing, joking, and enjoying one another.

One day I walked down to the pier to go sailing, and the little boat was gone. Somebody had taken my beautiful little sailboat. That boat was almost like a member of the family.

Several weeks later I was driving through the center part of Merritt Island where we lived, and I looked over at a marine shop. There on a special little mound was my boat. And it had a "For Sale" sign on it.

I went in the store to inquire about the boat, and the man told me the price. I asked him where he got the boat, and he said he was selling it for someone else. I informed him that it was my boat, and I was coming for it. He said, "Mister, you had better not touch that boat."

I went home and got my boat trailer. I came back to the marine shop and began to load the boat onto my trailer. The owner of the shop came out and said, "What are you doing?" I said, "I am taking my boat home. If you disagree with what I am doing, I suggest that you call the police." He turned and went inside. That's the last I saw of him. As you read this book, unless God has providentially intervened, that little boat is in my backyard.

Satan may bluff, but we need not be afraid. We need to keep our eyes focused and appropriate that which is already ours in Jesus Christ. And that which we have is Kingdom Authority!

PART I

Recognizing the Priority of Kingdom Authority

CHAPTER 1

OPEN YOUR EYES TO KINGDOM AUTHORITY

If we let passion take the place of judgment,
and self-will reign instead of Scriptural authority,
we shall fight the Lord's battles with the devil's weapons,
and if we cut our own fingers we must not be surprised.
—CHARLES HADDON SPURGEON

God wants his children to live as children of the King with Kingdom Authority. The whole matter is this: In order to live exercising authority over the world, the flesh, and the devil, *we must first submit to the authority that God has set over us.*

We will learn more of this principle later, but the problem of rebellion is very much a part of today's world. People don't like the idea of authority—Kingdom Authority or any other kind.

The word *authority* is an ugly word for many in today's society. It resonates with restriction, regulation, and control. Just the mention of the word can cause brows to narrow and scowls to form.

Resisting authority comes naturally to us because of Adam and Eve's rebellion against God in the Garden of Eden. And it intensifies with fervor today. A swell began to rise up in the ocean of ideas and philosophies in the 1960s. The Beatles sang of a revolution, and they got one—a revolution against authority. The slogans began to fly—"Resist Authority," "Question Authority," "Do Your Own Thing," "If It Feels Good, Do It." It was the "Me Generation."

The generations of the 1970s and 1980s rode the tide of the 1960s and the wave crested for the generation of the 1990s. The young people who grew up in these years will be remembered for many things—but in regard to man's rebellion, there can be no greater example than those who sought fame and recognition through killing sprees in the public school system. One of these murderous young men said, "My belief is that if I say something, it goes. I am the law. . . . I feel no remorse, no sense of shame."

Churning into a bona fide tidal wave of rebellion, this revolution hit the shores of every home in America. And the shock waves are still washing over the lives of every family in America today.

The revolution of the 1960s was to liberate the traditional family. Women were supposed to be set free from their husbands, their homes, and their children. The husband was to be set free from responsibility and liberated from authority. Even the children were granted liberation from limits.

Everyone was set free from time-honored standards of morals and ethics. The alluring song of free love was heard across the land. And what did we get with all the freedom we espoused? Abandoned restraint and a loosening of family values. With the seeds we sowed in the 1960s, we now have a harvest of fatherless children, vile venereal diseases, runaway divorce rates, and a generation of jaded, unloved, and undisciplined kids.

Our high schools hand out condoms to students, and fifteen-year-old mothers wrestle with the idea of birth control implants to keep them from getting pregnant again. The sexual revolution has come full cycle. People talk about sex openly, all right. In fact, it's about all some people think about. Sex has become a sport—like an aerobic workout. Nobody, however, said there would be consequences. Consequences such as unwanted children, herpes, syphilis, gonorrhea, bacterial infections, fungus, lice, *and the biggest consequence of all: AIDS.*

The time has passed when young men and women save themselves for marriage as a matter of honor. Junior high virgins may even tell the lie that they are promiscuous, because to be a virgin is to be a misfit. It's a mark of shame for a fifteen-year-old to never have "gone all the way."

Indeed, God knew all along the result of the evil that rampaged through the morals of our society. His Word tells us, "Be not deceived; God is not mocked: for whatsoever a man soweth, that shall he also reap. For he that soweth to his flesh shall of the flesh reap corruption; but he that soweth to the Spirit shall of the Spirit reap life everlasting" (Gal. 6:7–8).

The cry for freedom of expression is really a form of rebellion that mocks beauty, truth, and culture. In the name of art, men and women are producing works that defame the deity of Christ, belittle the Christian institution of the family, and degrade the beauty of God's creation. Instead of music that is edifying and uplifting, many of today's music performers are writing lyrics saturated with violence, obscenity, vulgarity, and outright blasphemy. Much of today's music is basically pornography set to music.

The theme underlying it all is anti-authority. Instead of portraying police as the protectors of our community, they are portrayed as freeloaders at doughnut shops. Instead of fathers who lovingly care for and support their families, we have television programs that make a mockery of fatherhood, and of parenthood and healthy marital relationships as well.

What is the end result of a generation that cuts its teeth on anti-authority rhetoric? Rebels and revolutionaries at worst. "Closet rebels" at best. It's very difficult to be a part of today's society and not be affected. I am afraid there is a little rebel in each of us.

We are in a crisis of monumental proportions—*it is an authority crisis.* Jesus prophesied that the last days will be marked by a spirit of lawlessness (Matt. 24:1–12). Indeed, our generation has seen the fulfillment of that ominous prophecy.

Our only hope is in discovering the Kingdom Authority that Jesus offers his children. I'm not talking about *mere* power, but authority. Many Christians today talk about having the power to overcome evil. That's not enough. Don't confuse authority with power.

Jesus made the distinction in Luke 9:1 when he gave the disciples power and authority over the satanic forces of wickedness. As in the passage we saw earlier from Luke 10, the Greek word here for "power" is *dunamis,* which means ability and strength, and the Greek word for "authority" is *exousia,* which means the official right. Authority is conferred; power is innate.

The Pharisees of Jesus' day boasted of their position in the kingdom of God and questioned what Jesus meant by the freedom we have as believers: "They answered him, We be Abraham's seed, and were never in bondage to any man: how sayest thou, Ye shall be made free? Jesus answered them, Verily, verily, I say unto you, Whosoever committeth sin is the servant of sin. And the servant abideth not in the house for ever: but the Son abideth ever. If the Son therefore shall make you free, ye shall be free indeed" (John 8:33–36).

With Kingdom Authority comes freedom, not bondage. These Pharisees who were vassals of Rome and slaves to sin were boasting about freedom. They were not free but slaves. The rebel is free to do what he wants within limits, but he is never free to do what he ought without Kingdom Authority operating in him. He is free to choose as he wishes, but he is not free to choose the consequences of that choice. He may show his freedom to choose by stepping out of a window of a skyscraper. At that point, however, he is not free to choose the consequences of that choice. The choice then chooses for him.

The paradoxical truth is that the freedom and authority we have in Jesus is because we are under authority. Let me illustrate. The train that runs with incredible speed on ribbons of steel is far freer to be what it was *made to be* than a so-called free train that may choose an excursion through the meadow. It is only free to wreck. A train is made to run on tracks, not in the green glades along the tracks.

When we wrap our arms around this truth, we will be set free and filled with joy as the psalmist who said, "Thy statutes have been my songs in the house of my pilgrimage" (Ps. 119:54). The law of God is a song in our life. The late, great Dr. Vance Havner had this to say:

> One does not ordinarily associate law books with song-books, mandates with music. But here's a man to whom the law of the Lord is no burdensome thing, a pattern of hard lines. Here's a radiant believer to whom law is liberty and service like unto a happy song.
>
> One may be good in such a bad way. Some of us have punctiliously kept the statutes but have failed to sing the songs. We have whiteness but no light. The Christian life does have its stern, unyielding requirements; but every law has a song written on the back and between the requirements runs the refrain. Duty turns to delight and mandates become melodies.
>
> There must be a law if there is to be liberty. Try to play a piano and you will run into laws as fixed as the decrees of the Medes and Persians. But through those statutes you reach the songs, drudgery leads to delight. The law of Christ brings the liberty of Christ. Keep His statutes, and they become songs. The other side of commandment is conquest. What seems restraint to the outsider means release to you.
>
> "Ye shall know the truth"—there are the statutes. "The truth shall make you free"—there is the song. But to know the truth is to know Him, otherwise it is legalism. If the Son shall make you free, ye shall be free indeed. His law book becomes a song book!

THE MISSING MIRACLE

Ours is a supernatural faith built around three personal miracles. Our faith *commences* with a miracle. We come into the kingdom by a miraculous new birth (John 3:3). Our salvation *concludes* with a miracle. At our Lord's coming we will be made like him (1 John 3:2). What a transformation! But there is the *continuing middle miracle* that many seem to miss. This miracle is that we can reign in life right now with Kingdom Authority.

Christians are not just nice people. They are new creatures with spiritual royalty. They are not like a tadpole graduating into a frog but are more like a frog transformed by the kiss of grace to become a prince. "For if by one man's offence death reigned by one; much more they which receive abundance of grace and of the gift of righteousness shall reign in life by one, Jesus Christ" (Rom. 5:17).

But what kind of a king can reign without authority? None! In the same way, we cannot reign in the grace and power of our Lord without Kingdom Authority.

The life that God desires for us is to be one of divine Kingdom Authority. While the Bible admits the possibility of defeat for a Christian, it never assumes the necessity of it. We are already kings and priests meant to live in perpetual victory—not necessarily in ease, wealth, or health but victory. Kingdom Authority is not only for the "sweet by and by" but for the believer today. It is your birthright and legacy.

Satan will marshal all the forces of hell and the demons of darkness to keep you in ignorance about your Kingdom Authority. Satan wants to deceive you into thinking that victory is impossible—even if you are swimming in an ocean of potential blessing!

A friend told about an experiment he had seen in a film. A large walleye pike was taken alive and placed in a huge aquarium. The water temperature and surroundings were adjusted to match the lake he was taken from. Then, buckets of live minnows were dumped in. Mr. Pike thought he was in heaven. He began rapidly swallowing these minnows.

A short while later, the researchers played a trick on the fish. They placed a large glass cylinder of water into the tank, then filled it with minnows. Mr. Pike started for the minnows again, only to bump his snout against the invisible barrier. He tried again and again and again. Finally he gave up and settled on the bottom of his "heaven" that had gone awry.

The researchers then removed the cylinder, and the minnows swam freely in the tank. But Mr. Pike never made a move for one of them. They would swim right past his face, but he never moved. He was convinced that he would never have another minnow. He finally starved, surrounded by minnows.

Have you ever thought that you may be asking God for what you already have? It is time for you to open your eyes and possess your possessions. Are you saved? Have you repented of your sin, believed upon Jesus Christ to save you, and made him Lord of your life? Then you are a member of the royal family of God with Kingdom Authority!

Simon Peter tells us, "According as his divine power hath given unto us all things that pertain unto life and godliness, through the knowledge of him that hath called us to glory and virtue: Whereby are given unto us exceeding great and precious promises: that by these ye might be partakers of the divine nature, having escaped the corruption that is in the world through lust" (2 Pet. 1:3–4). One of these days, we're going to wake up and understand what God has already given his children and stop asking him for what we already have. Living victoriously isn't your *responsibility;* it is rather your *response* to God's ability.

We are conquerors *through* Christ. Romans 8:35–37 says: "Who shall separate us from the love of Christ? shall tribulation, or distress, or persecution, or famine, or nakedness, or peril, or sword? As it is written, For thy sake we are killed all the day long; we are accounted as sheep for the slaughter. Nay, in all these things *we are more than conquerors through him that loved us.*" The key in this passage is the word "through." How do we have Kingdom Authority? Through Christ. Behind every promise is a person. And his name is Jesus.

As believers, we should walk on conquered ground. Stake your claim of faith on the promises of God. And do as Winston Churchill once said: "Never give in, never give in, never, never, never, never."

CHAPTER 2

GETTING READY FOR THE WAR

ASSAILING SATAN'S STRONGHOLDS

There is a *cosmic* battle raging, and it's a fight to the death with no holds barred. Ephesians 6:12 says, "For our struggle is not against flesh and blood, but against the rulers, against the authorities, against the powers of this dark world and against the spiritual forces of evil in the heavenly realms" (NIV). We are at *spiritual* war!

Therefore, the church is not a cruise ship with the pastor as the master of ceremonies. Indeed it is not a *showboat,* but a *battleship.* We're called to see Satan's strongholds crumble under the power of heaven's artillery.

We do not have the luxury of neutrality. We must engage in the fight. A truce will never be called. God's will for his saints is *not that we merely survive,* but that we *thrive in total victory.*

General Douglas MacArthur spoke rightly when he said, "In war there is no substitute for victory." We must be aware of our enemy if we would have this victory. We need to learn of our infernal foe.

MORE ABOUT THE ENEMY

If you want more insight into the origin and destination of Satan, study Ezekiel 28. In this chapter, the king of ancient Tyrus is used as an illustration or type of Satan himself. He was wicked indeed, but Satan was the power behind his throne—energizing all manner of evil under the pretense that it was the king orchestrating the evil deeds.

In Scripture, we find that God often addressed Satan through third parties, such as animals and men. God spoke to Satan when he took the form of a serpent in Eden (see Gen. 3:14–15). Jesus rebuked Satan when he took the form of man in Simon Peter. This was when Simon Peter attempted to stand between Jesus and the cross (see Matt. 16:22–23). Satan is not the figment of our imagination or the mere personification of evil. He is for real!

SATAN WAS CREATED IN PERFECTION

Ezekiel 28:12–13 says, "Son of man, take up a lamentation upon the king of Tyrus, and say unto him, Thus saith the Lord GOD; Thou sealest up the sum, full of wisdom, and *perfect in beauty.* Thou hast been in Eden the garden of God; every precious stone was thy covering, the sardius, topaz, and the diamond, the beryl, the onyx, and the jasper, the sapphire, the emerald, and the carbuncle, and gold: the workmanship of thy tabrets and of thy pipes was prepared in thee in the day that thou wast created." When Satan was created, he was surpassing in beauty and superlative in wisdom.

When he spoke, his voice cascaded like a crescendo of a great organ. He was the highest class of angel who lived in a jeweled city on the holy mount (in the Old Testament, a mountain stands for Kingdom Authority). Along with his privilege and beauty, he was given authority. Also, Ezekiel 28:18 mentions sanctuaries, indicating that Satan was involved in the worship of Almighty God. What honor and perfection belonged to him!

SATAN WAS CORRUPTED THROUGH PRIDE

Some people ask, "Why did God create the devil?" The answer is that God did not create the devil. God created a holy angel and gave that angel the power of choice. Along with his perfection, the devil received *perfect freedom*. The tragedy is that he fell! Despite his privilege, his position, and his power, he chose pride. And it is this one thing, pride, that makes the devil the devil. Ezekiel 28:15–19 records the fall of the devil in this way:

> Thou [Satan] wast perfect in thy ways from the day that thou wast created, till iniquity was found in thee. By the multitude of thy merchandise they have filled the midst of thee with violence, and thou hast sinned: therefore I will cast thee as profane out of the mountain of God: and I will destroy thee, O covering cherub, from the midst of the stones of fire. Thine heart was lifted up because of thy beauty, thou hast corrupted thy wisdom by reason of thy brightness: I will cast thee to the ground, I will lay thee before kings, that they may behold thee. Thou hast defiled thy sanctuaries by the multitude of thine iniquities, by the iniquity of thy traffic; therefore will I bring forth a fire from the midst of thee, it shall devour thee, and I will bring thee to ashes upon the earth in the sight of all them that behold thee. All they that know thee among the people shall be astonished at thee: thou shalt be a terror, and never shalt thou be any more.

Isaiah called him Lucifer: "How art thou fallen from heaven, O Lucifer, son of the morning! how art thou cut down to the ground, which didst weaken the nations" (Isa. 14:12). *Lucifer* means "light bearer." Lucifer, the son of the morning, became Satan, the father of the night. And why? Pride! Satan determined to "be like the most High" (Isa. 14:14). Yet he will be made the lowest of the low because *pride is the most devilish attribute that anyone may possess.*

SATAN CONTINUES WITH POWER

As soon as Satan unsheathed his sword of rebellion, he was swiftly banished from heaven (see Luke 10:18). Though he no longer has a position in heaven, he is still allowed limited power on earth, through deception and craft. To those who do not know the power of their God-given Kingdom Authority over Satan, the story is tragic indeed.

In Mark 5:1–20, we read the story of a man whom Jesus delivered from a swarm of demons living within him. The story is a classic example of Satan's ultimate design in his war against the human race—to completely inhabit, torment, and damn a human soul to hell. In this man we see the *power of Satan crystallized in human form.* Therefore, this man is a microcosm of all of Satan's destructive warfare:

> And they came over unto the other side of the sea, into the country of the Gadarenes. And when he [Jesus] was come out of the ship, immediately there met him out of the tombs a man with an unclean spirit, who had his dwelling among the tombs; and no man could bind him, no, not with chains: because that he had been often bound with fetters and chains, and the chains had been plucked asunder by him, and the fetters broken in pieces: neither could any man tame him. And always, night and day, he was in the mountains, and in the tombs, crying, and cutting himself with stones.
>
> But when he saw Jesus afar off, he ran and worshipped him, and cried with a loud voice, and said, What have I to do with thee, Jesus, thou Son of the most high God? I adjure thee by God, that thou torment me not. For he said unto him, Come out of the man, thou unclean spirit. And he asked him, What is thy name? And he answered, saying, My name is Legion: for we are many (Mark 5:1–9).

Notice what Satan had done to this pitiful man. He was crazed and tormented, full of rage and covered in dirt. When we see what the power of Satan can do in a person's life, then we can understand a little bit more what is happening to our age in this decade of demons. Let's take a closer look at the corresponding signs that revealed the destructive power of Satan in his life.

Preoccupation with Death. First, Legion had a *preoccupation with death.* All you have to do is look at where he lived. His dwelling was among the tombs. Legion wasn't in a hospital with ill people; he was in a cemetery with dead people! Where does Satan want his converts? In the chambers of the dead. Satan is the sinister minister of death.

In John 10:9–10, Jesus contrasted himself with Satan. He said, "I am the door: by me if any man enter in, he shall be saved, and shall go in and out, and find pasture. *The thief cometh not, but for to steal, and to kill, and to destroy:* I am come that they might have life, and that they might have it more abundantly." How can the murderous ways of society and the preoccupation with death be explained apart from the influence of Satan?

The rock music culture of our youth is thriving on Satan's dance with death. Look at the list below. Would you believe that these are the names of rock bands? Names of groups like these can be found in record stores and in music magazines:

Anthrax, Autopsy, Biohazard, Blood Feast, Blue Murder,
Brain Sick, Cannibal Corpse, Carcass, Carnivore, Cemetery
Club, Christian Death, The Damned, Dark Angel, Deceased,
Demolition, Demonic Christ, Destruction, Devastation,
Embalmer, Excrement, Fleshcrawl, Grim Reaper, Kill for
Thrills, Massacre, Megadeath, Necrophobic, Pestilence, Rigor
Mortis, Rotting Christ, Septic Flesh, Slaughter, Suicide Kings,
Vampire Rodents

Rebellion against Authority. Legion could not be tamed. Neither education nor psychology had any effect on this man. One might as well throw snowballs at the Rock of Gibraltar with hope of removing it as to use these humanistic methods to reform the static spirit of rebellion in this wild human heart. His spirit was one of utter defiance.

In addition, Legion could not be bound. Mark 5:3b–4 says, "No man could bind him, no, not with chains: because that he had been often bound with fetters and chains, and the chains had been plucked asunder by him, and the fetters broken in pieces." Our jails overflow with rebels, who like this man are bound with fetters and chains, only to rebel all the more when they escape or when they are released.

Uncleanness and Nudity. The demons, called "unclean spirits," had stripped this man of any sense of dignity and decency. They didn't care about this man's modesty. They kept him naked—completely exposed to the elements of the weather and the repercussions of his own tormented soul.

That's how Satan works. He removes all sense of decency as part of his plan to destroy. Indeed, ours is a generation of unblushables with a satanic fixation on nudity. All sense of modesty and restraint has been taken away. Advertisements and movies are filled with images of women and men unashamedly displaying their bodies. Some have faces like angels but morals like alley cats. They have been encaptured by the same spirit that dwelt in this man so long ago.

The power of Satan is an unclean power. Many who follow him use the language of the gutter. Filthy language that was brewing in the heart now belches even from the mouths of today's children. Where do they learn this kind of talk? They are merely repeating what they have seen and heard from a satanically controlled media that has corrupted their impressionable mentality.

Restlessness and Sadness. Mark 5:5 says, "And always, night and day, he [Legion] was in the mountains, and in the tombs, crying, and cutting himself with stones." The way of the transgressor is hard. Our choices, either willingly or passively, can cause us great heartache and pain.

Look at today's generation, heartbroken and under siege by Satan. We have prosperity but no peace. We seek peace from a bottle, a pill, or a syringe. Yet our mental hospitals are full. Psychiatrists, insurance companies, and for-profit mental institutions are getting rich while their patients are sinking deeper into despondency and despair. Why?

Because they're treating the outward symptoms and not where the true disease rages—in the heart which is "deceitful above all things, and desperately wicked" (Jer. 17:9).

Self-mutilation and Destructive Acts. The tormented man described in Mark took sharp stones and cut himself. Where did he learn to do this? Where else but the demons? They had him in their control.

I am amazed to see a modern generation moving more and more into self-mutilation. And I don't mean that they are all cutting on themselves with stones, knives, or other sharp objects (though many teenagers are in therapy today because of self-mutilating behavior).

And who can explain body piercing? Look at what many "wholesome" young men and women are doing with their bodies—piercing them with pins, common nails, and other objects. Dare anyone say this is normal or natural? And this is relatively mild behavior compared to the weird forms of sexual torture, occult behavior, self-destructive drug abuse, and suicide that are escalating in our society. These are a part of the demonic activity in Satan's modern war against mankind.

I visited a beautiful young girl who had attempted suicide by an overdose of drugs. She had given herself over to Satan. It was pitiful to see how she had carved satanic symbols into her arms and abdomen. I thank God that by prayer she was delivered and raised up. My hope is that she is living now in victory. I will never forget, however, the horror of seeing a beautiful girl who had willingly carved satanic symbols into her own flesh.

Separation from Family and Friends. When the possessed man was finally delivered, he wanted to go with Jesus, but Jesus told him, "Go home to thy friends, and tell them how great things the Lord hath done for thee, and hath had compassion on thee" (Mark 5:19). This reaction from Jesus tells me that the enemy had stolen the joy and fellowship that his family and friends should know.

Family and friends can bring us the highest happiness, exceeded only by our personal relationship with God. But, remember who our enemy is? He is one who seeks "to steal, and to kill, and to destroy"

(John 10:10). Satan brings domestic violence, separation, arguments, and strife into these relationships. These are all weapons in his arsenal.

Hostility to the Lord Jesus Christ. "But when he [Legion] saw Jesus afar off, he ran and worshipped him, and cried with a loud voice, and said, What have I to do with thee, Jesus, thou Son of the most high God? I adjure thee by God, that thou torment me not" (Mark 5:6–7). This man saw Jesus from far away and ran to him and worshiped him! Does this sound like a man tormented by demons? Yes, if you look through his eyes of fear and negativism. The demons were hostile to Jesus.

We are a generation today that does not so much *ignore* Jesus as it *hates* him.

I was in an airport one day and noticed a girl pinning small American flags on soldiers. I was deeply grieved when I observed her because she exuded an air of seduction. She wasn't just pinning American flags on them; she was trying to *charm them* into taking some propaganda from her false cult.

I was hoping she would speak to me so I could witness to her. When I didn't get her attention, I moved to her and asked, "May I tell you something?" "Yes," she replied. I then looked her straight in the face and said, "Jesus Christ is Lord." At that she let out a blood-curdling scream that filled the entire airport. One would have thought I had driven a wooden stake through her heart. Satan and his demons have a dread of Jesus, and so do those inhabited by him.

This ought to let us know something of the battle we're fighting. And we must wage war against this enemy with an understanding and application of Kingdom Authority. Second Chronicles 20:15 gives us this promise: "For the battle is not yours, but God's."

SATAN IS CONDEMNED TO PERDITION

Ezekiel 28:18 says, "Thou hast defiled thy sanctuaries by the multitude of thine iniquities, by the iniquity of thy traffic; therefore will I bring forth a fire from the midst of thee, it shall devour thee, and I will bring thee to ashes upon the earth in the sight of all them that behold thee."

Thank God that when Satan said in his arrogance, "I will ascend," Jesus in his humility and humanity said, "I will descend." Jesus, through his death, burial, and resurrection, has conquered. "Forasmuch then as the children are partakers of flesh and blood, he also himself likewise took part of the same; that through death he might destroy [*katargeō*] him that had the power of death, that is, the devil" (Heb. 2:14).

Katargeō means to make of none effect. This is what Jesus did at Calvary. When he was on the cross, hell had a holiday. Those jeering at him were saying, "He is finished." Yet Jesus was not finished. To the contrary, Jesus said, "It is finished." It was the plan of redemption that was finished. And through death, Jesus destroyed him who had the power of death.

Here is the conquest of Calvary. "And having spoiled principalities and powers, he made a show of them openly, triumphing over them in it" (Col. 2:15). To *spoil* something means to strip the hide from an animal or to disarm and strip the medals from a defeated foe. Satan and his kingdom are thrown into complete bankruptcy by the resurrection. His dominion has been dissolved.

While Satan may not have vanished, he has been vanquished. Ours is the victory. "Ye are of God, little children, and have overcome them: because greater is he that is in you, than he that is in the world" (1 John 4:4).

We look forward to that final, glorious, triumphant day when Jesus as King of kings is enthroned over the earth and Satan will be cast into hell. The one who walked back and forth in the stones of fire will descend into the lake of fire. Then the utter folly, the sheer stupidity, of following this king of terrors will be made manifest. The saints will be given a future position greater than the position that Satan had before he fell. This is why I often say, "I had rather be a saved sinner than an innocent angel."

There are two kings that seek the allegiance of mankind this day—the King of kings and the king of terrors. Why follow a loser?

CHAPTER 3

TAKING BACK LOST GROUND

Kingdom authority was gloriously given to us by God,
then legally lost by the first Adam, and
righteously regained by the second Adam—
the Son of God, our Lord Jesus Christ!

I serve on the board of Focus on the Family, which is headquartered in Colorado Springs, Colorado. One of my fellow board members is General Patrick Caruana, who is a high-ranking official in America's Strategic Space Command.

While in Colorado Springs for a meeting one year, I joined General Caruana for a tour of the facilities there. I was amazed at the scope of America's space technology. Did you know that America has satellites in synchronous orbit above the earth that can look down into the backyards of every nation with precision?

Every backyard of *every* nation. Now, that's a powerful weapon in warfare! General Caruana explained that from ancient times warfare has been won by taking the high ground.

I got to see some of this "high ground" during my tour. General Caruana led me to a room where I saw Libya on a screen. Little lights were flashing all over the cities of this nation. The young man who was performing this operation told us, "We can tell if a missile is fired, and we can plot its trajectory and its arrival time with precision." I asked about the technology. With a twinkle in his eye, he said, "It's top secret. If I were to tell you, I would have to kill you."

But the wonderful truth of our *spiritual* high ground is no secret. It's a liberating truth that God has freely given us—Kingdom Authority power! The power that the church of Ephesus had as children of God! The same power that we have today as children of the King of kings! Paul exhorted the believers of Ephesus to see that they could lay claim to all the rights of the kingdom of God—just as we can if we will only believe!

"Oh, God! Help them know of the power that is involved here. Let them understand what is available to them through the work of Christ! And, Lord, help me, too, that in my preaching I might always help God's people understand it." It was the cry of Paul's heart while imprisoned in a dark prison cell in Rome.

Imprisoned, yet not without a voice, Paul fervently labored in prayer and wrote letters of encouragement and exhortation to the many churches to which he was ministering. And he was to discover that his efforts were not in vain.

Word came that God's Spirit had broken loose in Ephesus and that the Ephesians were giving themselves to Christ in great numbers! Ephesians 1:15–16 gives us Paul's exact words: "Wherefore I also, after I heard of your faith in the Lord Jesus, and love unto all the saints, cease not to give thanks for you, making mention of you in my prayers."

Sounds like this was the good news for which he was praying and that he could let up a little on his intense labor. Right? Wrong! The people exhibited faith in the Lord Jesus, and they loved each other, but Paul wasn't satisfied. He kept on praying. What else could he pray for? Let's eavesdrop on the prayers of a saint as we read further:

That the God of our Lord Jesus Christ, the Father of glory, may give unto you the spirit of wisdom and revelation in the knowledge of him: The eyes of your understanding being enlightened; that ye may know what is the hope of his calling, and what the riches of the glory of his inheritance in the saints, And what is the exceeding greatness of his power to us-ward who believe, according to the working of his mighty power, Which he wrought in Christ, when he raised him from the dead, and set him at his own right hand in the heavenly places, far *above all principality, and power, and might, and domin-ion, and every name that is named,* not only in this world, but also in that which is to come: and hath put all things under his feet, and gave him to be the head over all things to the church, which is his body, the fulness of him that filleth all in all (Eph. 1:17–23).

Paul wanted the church in Ephesus to keenly understand "the exceeding greatness of his power" to us. He wanted them to believe in that *power* that reached down into a tomb near Jerusalem two thousand years ago, raised Christ from death to life, and brought him homeward to rule in the heavens (v. 20). That this almighty *power* now rules the rulers of heaven and earth (v. 21). And, that they must now draw on that *power* by which everything has been placed under the feet of Christ, who now rules the church as his own body (vv. 22–23). The power *behind us* and that is *in us* comes from *above us.* Paul wanted the Ephesians to have their eyes opened to this incredible power.

Dwell on these words: "Power . . . working . . . strength . . . might." All hell had marshaled its forces against the resurrection. Had Jesus stayed in that grave, Satan would have prevailed. The victory of the empty tomb was the stroke that brought the kingdom of death and hell crashing down.

Now, don't miss this. This same resurrection power is given "to us-ward who believe" (v. 19). Since Jesus died for us, we died with him. He rose for us and we are raised with him. His death, burial, and resurrec-tion had our name on it. We are a part of his resurrection body. The head and the body are raised together. He is the head, and we are the feet. What is under his headship is also under our feet.

Jesus is enthroned on high, above all principalities and powers. We, in our identification with him, are seated there with him. Don't miss this. "But God, who is rich in mercy, for his great love wherewith he loved us, even when we were dead in sins, hath *quickened us together with Christ,* (by grace ye are saved;) and hath *raised us up together, and made us sit together in heavenly places in Christ Jesus*" (Eph. 2:4–6).

Does this sound too wonderful to be true? Dare we presume such a thing? Indeed, we can. This is the secret of spiritual authority and the key to victory in spiritual warfare. To share a throne means to partake of the authority which that throne represents.

Satan also has his principalities and powers. "For we wrestle not against flesh and blood, but against principalities, against powers, against the rulers of the darkness of this world, against spiritual wickedness in high places" (Eph. 6:12).

- "Principalities and powers" speak of his *devilish dominion.*
- "Rulers of the darkness of this world" speak of his *devilish deception.*
- "Spiritual wickedness in high places" speaks of his *devilish destruction.*

Satan also rules from "the heavenlies"—that is, the sphere of spiritual activity. While he is in his lofty position, Jesus, however, is far above. "*Far above* all principality, and power, and might, and dominion, and every name that is named, not only in this world, but also in that which is to come" (Eph. 1:21). Remember that we fight from the highest ground. There are three tremendous truths that we must learn.

KINGDOM AUTHORITY WAS GLORIOUSLY GIVEN

The first truth we should learn about Kingdom Authority is that this authority was gloriously given to the first man, our ancestor Adam. We know this from Genesis 1:26, where we read that God created the first man and the first woman. He placed them in the Garden of Eden. "And God said, Let us make man in our image, after our likeness: and *let them have dominion*" (Gen. 1:26). God gave Adam dominion over the earth, which means to "tread down" or "to rule." The things of earth were intended to be under the feet of Adam and Eve. They were the appointed king and queen of the earth. "The heaven, even the heavens, are the LORD's: but the earth hath he given to the children of men" (Ps. 115:16).

Many years later, David, the singer of Psalms, commented on the dominion God gave man over his creation. Perhaps while gazing into the heavens on a starry night, David asked, "When I consider thy heavens, the work of thy fingers, the moon and the stars, which thou hast ordained; what is man, that thou art mindful of him? and the son of man, that thou visitest him?" (Ps. 8:3–4). As if David knew the answer to the question even before he asked, he continued: "Thou *madest him to have dominion over the works of thy hands;* thou hast put all things under his feet" (v. 6).

Adam was given dominion, but he lost it. And the bitter fruits of that loss are being harvested throughout our world today. Death, disease, hate, crime, pain, sorrow, and despair run rampant in the streets of our cities. A small boy sat on the front steps of his school crying. He was to bring his birth certificate to school, and his mother had told him to handle this critical document with care. A passerby asked him why he was crying. He sobbed, "I've lost my excuse for being born." A worse thing happened to Adam: he squandered God's reason for creating him.

Kingdom Authority Was Legally Lost

Not only was this dominion or authority *gloriously given;* it was *legally lost.* As we will see, it was also *foolishly lost.* It was Adam's possession, and he gave it away. He legally lost his Kingdom Authority. Adam took the dominion that God had given him and turned it over to Satan. That's what the third chapter of Genesis is all about—how Satan disguised himself as a serpent and crawled his corroding path into the pages of history and deceived the first man and the first woman.

Did you know that the Hebrew word for *serpent* also denotes "shining one"? And that the name *Lucifer* means "light bearer"? God never created a devil. He created a holy angel, a particularly beautiful one who *on his own* chose to rebel. God allowed him the freedom to choose. Lucifer, the son of the morning, became Satan, the father of the night, and was banished from heaven to earth, where he would try again to enthrone himself (see Ezek. 28:14–19; Isa. 14:13–14). But in order to do so, he had to usurp the dominion of the one who held it there—Adam.

How did all of this happen?

Satan came into the Garden of Eden with his *own religion.* Satan is not opposed to religion. It is a major weapon in his arsenal. The aim of his religion is to be "as God" (see Gen. 3:5). First, Satan came to Adam and Eve and began to spread his theology of lies about God: "Hath God said, Ye shall *not* eat of every tree of the garden?" (v. 1). The truth is that God said, "Of every tree of the garden thou *mayest freely eat:* but of the tree of the knowledge of good and evil, thou shalt not eat of it: for in the day that thou eatest thereof thou shalt surely die" (Gen. 2:16–17). Satan *was wanting Eve to think negatively about God.* He was attempting to plant the seed of rebellion in her heart.

It was really a temptation to "fall up," not down. She could be "as God." God said Adam and Eve would die if they ate from the tree of the knowledge of good and evil. But the "good news" (gospel) of Satan's religion was: "Ye shall not surely die: for God doth know that in the day ye eat thereof, then your eyes shall be opened, and ye shall be as gods, knowing good and evil" (Gen. 3:4–5). Satan planted the seed of doubt, then waited to see if Adam and Eve would take the next step of disbelief. We all know the rest of the story. Adam and Eve did not become a god like Satan promised. Instead they became Satan's slave.

Adam had been given authority. He did not have to yield to Satan's lie. He could have banished the serpent from the garden with the authority that he had over every beast of the field, but he failed to exercise it. He was "to keep" or protect the garden, but instead he lost it by default. Like the prodigal son, he squandered his legacy.

There is something about sin that makes it contagious. Sinners have an unholy desire to share their sin. Eve became Satan's evangelist, and she shared the devil's gospel with Adam. He was her first convert into the kingdom of evil.

When Adam and Eve sinned, they died spiritually to God (Gen. 2:17). They were no longer God's servants. Adam and Eve were now Satan's slaves: "They themselves are the servants of corruption: for of *whom a man is overcome, of the same is he brought in bondage*" (2 Pet. 2:19).

The owner of a slave owns not only the slave but all that the slave possesses. Therefore, when Adam and Eve sinned and became Satan's bondslaves, they yielded to him their most prized possession—the dominion God had bestowed upon them over his creation. This is why Satan could make such a boast to Jesus concerning the world's kingdoms. "And the devil said unto him, All this power will I give thee, and the glory of them: for that is delivered unto me; and to whomsoever I will I give it" (Luke 4:6).

True to his nature, Satan wasn't all that interested in Adam's dominion on earth; he wanted God's throne in the highest heaven. Satan wants to steal what belongs to God—the worship, adoration, and service of God's children.

However, Satan did not get dominion over a paradise but over a creation that is now ruined. It is now a *kingdom with a curse*—bringing forth thorns, thistles, and death: "And unto Adam he said, Because thou hast hearkened unto the voice of thy wife, and hast eaten of the tree, of which I commanded thee, saying, Thou shalt not eat of it: cursed *is* the ground for thy sake; in sorrow shalt thou eat *of* it all the days of thy life; thorns also and thistles shall it bring forth to thee; and thou shalt eat the herb of the field" (Gen. 3:17–18).

Not only is the kingdom corrupted, but the king and queen of the earth are now corrupted as well. Before Adam sold out to Satan, his spirit was alive with the presence of his Lord. He enjoyed uninterrupted, perfect, and holy communion with God. He walked with him in the garden and spoke with God freely and without fear.

When Adam and Eve fell to the ploy of Satan's deception, they fell from the noble place of authority they enjoyed in God's creation. And they began to live in bondage, fear, and servitude to a new master— Satan. The prince of this world, Satan, was handed his throne by Adam, who foolishly forfeited it. What Satan had failed to do in heaven, he has temporarily achieved on earth.

Adam had been a holy temple with the Spirit of God abiding in him. But now, that temple was defiled by sin, and God left it desolate. Sin separates, and God moved out of Adam's spirit. The temple that was afire with the presence of God's glory, a manifestation of his heavenly glory on earth, is now spiritually void. The Lord went out of Adam, and because the Lord went out, the life went out as well. And when the life went out, the light went out.

- Adam was now without the LORD—depraved.
- Adam was now without the LIFE—dead.
- Adam was now without the LIGHT—darkened.

KINGDOM AUTHORITY IS RIGHTEOUSLY REGAINED

This poses a question: If Satan has done such awful damage— usurping what was meant for us and creating havoc in the world—why hasn't God done something about it? Why hasn't God stepped in to clean up the mess? If God did that, as of course he could, he would fix things, but not in the way that would fulfill his righteous law.

God has his own standard of righteousness, holiness, and justice. *If the world's dominion was legally lost, then it must be legally regained.* If authority was lost by a man, then it must be regained by a man. The power of Satan defeated the first man and must be destroyed by another man—Jesus!

Francis Schaeffer, a great writer and theologian, had this to say about God's solution: "God in His sheer power could have crushed Satan in his revolt by the use of that sufficient power. But because of God's character, justice came before the use of power alone. Therefore Christ died that justice, rooted in what God is, would be the solution."[1]

"For God so loved the world, that he gave his only begotten Son, that whosoever believeth in him should not perish, but have everlasting life. For God sent not his Son into the world to condemn the world; but that the world through him might be saved" (John 3:16–17). It took one man to undo the damage another man did. Jesus, the second Adam, came to regain what the first Adam lost (see 1 Cor. 15:21–22).

- Jesus came as he did (born of a virgin) to be what he was—*holy.* If he had been the son of Adam with Adam's nature, he would have been a sinner because in Adam all have sinned and died. He would have also been a slave, for the son of a slave is himself a slave (see Heb. 2:14).
- Jesus was what he was (holy) to do what he did—*redeem us.* He came as a sinless man, paying the full price for our transgression. He satisfied God's righteous and holy law and nullified all of Satan's rights to Adam's domain.
- Jesus did what He did (redeem us) that we might have forgiveness, cleansing, a new nature, and Kingdom Authority. He is the head of a brand-new race.
- Jesus was born of a virgin that we might be born again.
- Jesus became the Son of Man that we might become the sons and daughters of God.
- Jesus died in agony that we might live in victory.

All of history and humanity comes down to these two men, Adam and Christ. Every man, woman, and child is either in Adam or in Christ. If we choose the lot of Adam, we share in his fate—the way of death, judgment, and hell. But if we choose Christ, we share in his victory over Satan and death, and we share in his glorious reward of eternal fellowship with God.

Jesus had to become a man, take on flesh and blood, and die to deal fully with the consequences of what had befallen all of us. Nothing less than death could wipe away the blot of sin. And nothing less than the power of God could raise Christ from the dead. What Adam legally lost, we have righteously regained in the incarnation of Jesus Christ (God becoming flesh). "Even so we, when we were children, were in bondage under the elements of the world: but when the fulness of the time was come, God sent forth his Son, made of a woman, made under the law, to redeem them that were under the law, that we might receive the adoption of sons" (Gal. 4:3–5).

Remember that the Kingdom Authority Jesus won back was won by his manhood. "For as the Father hath life in himself; so hath he given to the Son to have life in himself; and hath given him authority to execute judgment also, *because he is the Son of man*" (John 5:26–27). Jesus had righteousness because he was God's Son, but he had authority on earth because he was the Son of Man, without sin.

We are all born into certain families and inherit certain qualities, from eye color to financial status. We have no choice about the status of our birth. It just happens. We all inherit the slave status that Adam first brought on himself and his descendants when he signed away his God-given dominion. But in the fullness of time we are given a new opportunity: adoption as God's children with all the birthrights of Kingdom Authority, righteously regained.

How did Jesus do this? First, it wasn't without cost. Because God is absolutely holy and pure, he couldn't just wave his divine hand and absolve the sin of man as if nothing ever happened. God's standards are absolute. Our ascent from slavehood to sainthood had to be accomplished legally. In other words, Jesus had to reclaim what Satan had seized. Sin had to be atoned. It must be done legally. God cannot overlook sin. It is said that when a guilty man is acquitted in court the judge is condemned. God is the chief justice of the supreme court of the universe. The death of Jesus has satisfied his just nature.

> By the which will we are sanctified through the offering of the body of Jesus Christ once for all. And every priest standeth daily ministering and offering oftentimes the same sacrifices, which can never take away sins: but this man, after he had offered one sacrifice for sins for ever, sat down on the right

hand of God; from henceforth expecting till his enemies be made his footstool. For by one offering he hath perfected for ever them that are sanctified (Heb. 10:10–14).

Satan wanted to come against the last Adam as he did the first one. He had to tempt Jesus as a man, not as God because God cannot be tempted.

Jesus knew his confrontation with the devil would come. Satan would not accede to defeat without a fight. Matthew 4:1–11 records the scene. Shortly after Jesus was anointed for ministry by his Father, the Spirit led him into the wilderness where he fasted for forty days. There Satan threw at him all the artillery of hell and every temptation that had ever confronted humanity. To Satan's dismay, what worked on the first Adam was now powerless before the Last Adam.

Jesus did not defeat Satan in the wilderness by pulling rank and using the powers he had brought from heaven. He executed no miracles in this battle. He defeated Satan not as God, but as perfect man. His two weapons were then, and are today, sufficient for our victory in spiritual warfare: the *Spirit of God* and the *Word of God.* Filled with the Spirit, he unsheathed the Word of God to answer every devilish challenge.

You may ask, "Adam was at a disadvantage, wasn't he? Did he have these weapons in the Garden of Eden?" Absolutely. John 1:1 tells us, "In the beginning was the Word, and the Word was with God, and the Word was God." Adam had the Word of God and the Spirit of God. He was in perfect communion with God before the fall.

The example of this victory was given in the wilderness temptation, and the contract for our liberation was completed on the cross at Golgotha. Kingdom Authority changed hands once again, legally reverting its power to all of us who are believers in Jesus Christ. We identify with him in his death, and we join with him in defeating that death and ascending to the Father. The laws of sin and death are no longer binding on us. "There is therefore now no condemnation to them which are in Christ Jesus, who walk not after the flesh, but after the Spirit. For the law of the Spirit of life in Christ Jesus hath made me free from the law of sin and death" (Rom. 8:1–2).

Can you see why Paul prayed for our eyes to be opened, that we might really understand this power? If that ever happens, buckle your seat belt—*all heaven will break loose!*

CHAPTER 4

DRESSED FOR THE BATTLE

In warfare, it is strategically vital to know your enemy. We dare not be ignorant in this conflict. Education is costly, but ignorance is devastating. Let's learn about our adversary the devil.

Jesus sent out seventy witnesses into the harvest field to reap souls, saying: "Go your ways: behold, I send you forth as lambs among *wolves*" (Luke 10:3). And when they returned they were ecstatic with joy and reported, "Lord, even the *demons* are subject to us in Your name" (Luke 10:17 NKJV).

When they said "in Your name," they were recognizing that the name of Jesus is the key. Jesus' name stands for authority. It is *Kingdom Authority* that fits us for the battle. And it is *Kingdom Authority* that will assure us *perpetual* victory.

The Bible admits the possibility of spiritual defeat in our warfare, but it never *assumes it.* The normal Christian life is meant to be one of *perpetual victory.* "Now thanks be unto God, which always causeth us to triumph in Christ, and maketh manifest the savour of his knowledge by us in every place" (2 Cor. 2:14).

The classic passage that discusses our preparation for battle with our infernal foe is Ephesians 6:10–20:

Finally, my brethren, be strong in the Lord, and in the power of his might. Put on the whole armour of God, that ye may be able to stand against the wiles of the devil. For we wrestle not against flesh and blood, but against principalities, against powers, against the rulers of the darkness of this world, against spiritual wickedness in high places. Wherefore take unto you the whole armour of God, that ye may be able to withstand in the evil day, and having done all, to stand. Stand therefore, having your loins girt about with truth, and having on the breastplate of righteousness; and your feet shod with the preparation of the gospel of peace; above all, taking the shield of faith, wherewith ye shall be able to quench all the fiery darts of the wicked. And take the helmet of salvation, and the sword of the Spirit, which is the word of God: praying always with all prayer and supplication in the Spirit, and watching thereunto with all perseverance and supplication for all saints; and for me, that utterance may be given unto me, that I may open my mouth boldly, to make known the mystery of the gospel, for which I am an ambassador in bonds: that therein I may speak boldly, as I ought to speak.

SATAN IS REAL, AND HE IS RUTHLESS

In Ephesians 6:11, our enemy is called the devil. As we saw earlier, he has many criminal aliases, and *devil* is only one of his names. He is also known as serpent, Belial, Beelzebub, and the prince of the power of the air.

Our sophisticated age scoffs at the idea of a devil and demons. And no wonder—it has always been Satan's purpose to pull the veil of darkness over his kingdom until one day with boldness he will remove the veil and seek to be worshiped.

Ephesians 6:11–12 says, "Put on the whole armour of God, that ye may be able to stand against the wiles of the devil. For we wrestle not against flesh and blood, but against principalities, against powers, against the rulers of the darkness of this world, against spiritual wickedness in high places."

HE IS SYSTEMATIC IN HIS WARFARE

What are the "wiles of the devil"? His ruthless and tyrannical modus operandi. *Wiles* in the Greek is the same word that we get our word *methodical* from. It is the Greek word *methodia*. You can be certain that Satan is cleverly, assuredly going about to destroy all that is wholesome and godly in your life. He has a strategic and systematic plan just for you.

HE IS SPIRITUAL IN HIS ESSENCE

Paul speaks of "spiritual wickedness." It will be a great day when we learn that all that is spiritual is not necessarily *holy*. The apostle John warns us that there are evil spirits, and we need to test the spirits: "Beloved, believe not every spirit, but try the spirits whether they are of God: because many false prophets are gone out into the world" (1 John 4:1). Our battle is not with flesh and blood. Satan shrewdly gets us to battle and wrestle with flesh and blood, and then he smirks on the sidelines untouched while he enjoys our fight with one another.

HE IS STRONG IN HIS ABILITIES

May God forbid that we speak casually or lightly about Satan. When Paul speaks of "principalities and powers," he is not referring to a force that is easily subdued. A weak person is no match for this champion of darkness. Indeed, Martin Luther said it well in the first verse of his hymn, "A Mighty Fortress Is Our God":

> A mighty fortress is our God,
> A bulwark never failing;
> Our helper He amid the flood
> Of mortal ills prevailing.
> For still our ancient foe

Doth seek to work us woe—
His craft and power are great
And, armed with cruel hate,
On earth is not his equal.

HE IS SINISTER IN HIS MOTIVES

In Ephesians 6:12, Paul tells us that we wrestle against "the rulers of the darkness of this world, against spiritual wickedness in high places." Satan is *unspeakably wicked* and *devilishly devious*. Even when he appears as an angel of light, he is hideous and hateful in his heart.

How is this worked out today? Here are a few examples among hundreds to show you what we are up against.

First, there is a *frontal attack* from Satan that denies God and Bible morals. A recent letter to the editor in *USA Today* asked this question: "What does morality have to do with sexual behavior. . . . How can anyone say that an act between consenting adults that hurts no one is immoral? I frequently hear people denounce certain sexual behaviors as immoral; I don't get it. Webster defines moral as 'relating to principles of right or wrong.' How can a consensual sexual act be damaging to a 'principle of right'? . . . Morality has absolutely nothing to do with what, if any, God you believe in, what ethnicity you are, whether you drink or smoke, how old you are, whom you love, or what turns you on sexually." The truth is that this writer is correct if there is no God or we have created our own God.

Then there's a more *subtle attack* that is made on the impressionable minds of kids. My righteous indignation came to a boiling point when I read an advertisement printed in a skateboard magazine for kids. A full-page ad showed a cartoon of a smiley-faced devil with horns and holding a pitchfork saying, "Let's make a deal." There were a series of cartoon panels in the ad. Here is some of the dialog along with sexually suggestive art:

"Hi, kiddie, it's me, Devil Man. Along with my trusty sycophant, Flame Boy, here to make you a little offer. Here's the deal: I want your soul."

Then one of the demons addresses this smiley-faced devil with these words, "But boss, won't they need their souls if they wanna go to heaven? That's where I want to go when I die."

The devil replies, "First of all, Flame Boy, you're already dead and that's why you're in hell. And second of all, heaven is not all it's cracked up to be." He goes on to say, "I should know, I used to live there."

The little imp demon says, "You used ta live in heaven, Boss? I didn't know you used ta live there."

The devil goes on to explain, "You see, back when I lived up there, I tried to make heaven a fun place, but that just got me and my kids kicked out. Look how bad we were." And in this cartoon panel Satan has a bottle of booze and is surrounded by half-naked, seductive-looking women, and he has a skateboard under one arm.

Satan continues, "After God told me to go to hell, things in heaven were never quite the same. First of all, instead of a bunch of dumb rules, they imposed a really strict dress code. I wager that people must be quite bored up there, but hey, that's what they get for being good."

Without belaboring the point, let me tell you how this cartoon story ends. The devil tells his demon servant, "Flame Boy, even a dimwit like you can see that hell is by far the best place to retire. Just look at all the fun to be had. And remember, in hell there is only one rule, and that is there are no rules."

He concludes this with making a direct appeal, "So kids, to ensure your permanent place in hell, send me your soul right now. And just to make absolutely sure where you're going, it probably wouldn't hurt to buy a few of these things with my picture on them." And then there is an advertisement that says, "And if you act now and send in the following coupon releasing your soul to me for eternity, I'll send you this free T-shirt."

The last panel is a cut-out contract that says, "I, the undersigned, do hereby give possession of my soul to the devil, for eternity, for ever and ever and ever and ever and ever and ever and ever." And there is a place for the kids to sign their names and addresses. In the corner a smiling devil says, "I'll be seeing you."

Now, some may think this is very funny, but it makes my blood boil. Satan is made to look friendly and humorous, and God looks like a cosmic killjoy. All this aimed at the immature and still-pliable minds of kids with skateboards.

One more illustration—and remember, I could give you many, many more.

Satan, having captured the media and music, has gone after education. America's schoolchildren are under greater spiritual attack than ever before. Recently there was great concern about the Bedford, New York, Central School District, where New Age earth worship has come into full bloom. Bedford schools conducted elaborate Earth Day rituals that amounted to religious services. Students were even led in the recitation of this Earth Day creed, which exalts Gaia—Mother Earth:

> This is what we believe. The mother of us all is the earth.
> The father is the sun. The Grandfather is the Creator who
> made this with His mind and gave life to all things. The
> Brother is the beasts and trees. The sister is that with wings.
> We are children of the Earth and do it no harm in any way, nor
> do we offend the sun by not greeting it at dawn. We praise our
> Grandfather for his creation. We share the same birth
> together, beast, the trees, the birds, and the man.

The students were urged to present gifts to Mother Earth, and some students actually built altars for the Gaia worship ceremony. There you have it—from Father God to Mother Earth. Our children can't worship the true God in public schools, but they can worship dirt!

Satan is getting bolder and bolder. Yet, for the child of God, there can be victory. First John 4:4 promises, "Ye are of God, little children, and have overcome them: because greater is he that is in you, than he that is in the world."

THE CHRISTIAN SOLDIER AND HIS ARMOR

We are to put on the holy armor of God to fight this battle. And not just parts of the armor that we find convenient or useful at the time but the *whole* armor. We are foolish to go to war without being fully dressed for the battle.

Paul was familiar with the armor of a Roman soldier, as we can tell from his dramatic and detailed descriptions of "loins girt about with truth," "the breastplate of righteousness," "feet shod with the preparation of the gospel of peace," "the shield of faith," "the helmet of salvation," and "the sword of the Spirit."

THE BELT OF TRUTH—THE BELIEVER'S INTEGRITY

A soldier of that day wore a leather belt that held his armor together. It gave support to his solar plexus, and his other weapons hung from it. In the same way, we must have the truth of God holding us together. If we don't, Satan will work his devilish work of deception. After all, Jesus said, "When he [Satan] speaketh a lie, he speaketh of his own: for he is a liar, and the father of it" (John 8:44).

It is vitally important that you know the truth, believe the truth, tell the truth, and live the truth. Your life must be controlled by truth and integrity in this warfare. Satan will try to send fiery "lie-filled" darts your way. And if your armor is loose—not held together by the belt of truth—then that lie will find a way through your armor!

Remember that the cleverest lie sounds the most like the truth. It has often been said that a broken clock is right twice a day. Yet a clock five minutes wrong may be more dangerous than a clock five hours wrong. The clock five hours wrong is obviously wrong, while the clock five minutes wrong may cause you to miss the airplane.

THE BREASTPLATE OF RIGHTEOUSNESS—THE BELIEVER'S PURITY

The breastplate was made of metal plates or chains that covered the warrior's body from neck to waist. Its purpose was to protect the vital organs. In this passage, the breastplate symbolizes the believer's righteousness.

Satan is always looking for a crack in your armor so he can get at your heart. Impurity is that crack in the armor. Some small sin or lack of righteousness can make you vulnerable to Satan.

> "Who is it knocks so loud?"
> A lonely little sin.
> "Slip through," I answered.
> Soon all hell was in.

Proverbs 4:23 exhorts, "Keep thy heart with all diligence; for out of it are the issues of life." There is no reason whatsoever that you should not have an absolutely clean and pure heart at this very moment. If you need cleansing, simply ask God for his forgiveness. He is willing and ready to cleanse you from all sin.

THE SHOES OF PEACE—THE BELIEVER'S TRANQUILITY

The Roman soldiers wore sandals with hobnails on the bottom to give them sure footing. In this passage we're told to stand. And how are we to stand? In "feet shod with the preparation of the gospel of peace" (Eph. 6:15).

The battlefield will be rough. Satan will make sure it is full of thorns and briars and stumbling blocks. But the gospel of Jesus is the gospel of peace. He will give peace no matter how rocky the pathway and how sharp the thorns. Jesus promises, "These things I have spoken unto you, that in me ye might have peace. In the world ye shall have tribulation: but be of good cheer; I have overcome the world" (John 16:33). When we equip ourselves with the gospel of peace and move forward on the battlefield, we will leap rather than limp! There is peace in the midst of the battle.

THE SHIELD OF FAITH—THE BELIEVER'S CERTAINTY

The shield was generally made of wood and covered with leather. It was so strong that it would stop flaming arrows. A soldier in battle carried it with him at all times. He wouldn't think of carrying his sword without his shield. It was his defensive weapon in battle. In the same way, our faith is our defensive weapon against Satan's fiery darts of doubt.

Do you know what it feels like to have Satan fire his fiery darts of doubt at you? If you haven't experienced them, just wait—he'll fire them when you're least expecting it. If you have experienced them, you know they are set on fire in the very pit of hell. All it takes is a spark of doubt to start a great fire.

Who needs to take up the shield? Every child of God, and especially Christian college students who face the liberal, humanistic values of the world's universities. Christian business people need it, too. When their faith is tested in the workplace, will they stand firm, or will they throw down the shield of faith in defeat?

THE HELMET OF SALVATION—THE BELIEVER'S SANITY

The Roman warrior wore a helmet to protect his head. He wouldn't be any use to his battalion if he lost his head, would he? In the midst of a battle, soldiers have to maintain a cool head. They cannot "lose it." They must recall the things they've learned so they can apply them in the heat of combat—especially the basics about fighting the fight and winning the war.

In the same way, we need to put on the helmet of salvation so we can keep our head in the midst of the battle. We need to be firm in the promise of our salvation. In the midst of a battle, we must have our minds protected and controlled by God.

The devil wants to control your thought life because you are what you think. Many people have been taken snare by the devil simply because they have not controlled their thought life.

Are you ready for battle? What about your integrity, your purity, your tranquility, your certainty, your sanity? If you think about it, you'll see that all of these things are personified in the Lord Jesus Christ. Christ is our armor, and we are to be dressed up in him.

We are fools to go into battle without every piece of armor in place.

THE CHRISTIAN WARRIOR AND HIS ATTACK

It's not enough to be dressed fully in the armor. We must get into the battle offensively and wage war. It is not enough simply to defend ourselves against Satan. We need to stop singing "Hold the Fort" and begin singing "Onward Christian Soldiers." There are some key factors in this offensive battle that we wage.

THE PLACE OF OUR STANCE

We are to "stand therefore," and where do we stand? We're standing in victory already won. We have been given authority over Satan. Stop confessing the negatives about yourself or others, and start thanking God for what he is doing.

Rather than saying, "Lord, be with me," why not say, "Father, I know you are with me and will never forsake me." Rather than saying, "God, help me to have peace in this desperate time," instead say, "Father, you are my peace. I stand in the peace won at Calvary." Rather than saying, "Father, give me victory over Satan," say, "Lord, I am standing in victory that you won at Calvary."

This is a lesson the Israelites had to learn. When they had fled Egypt and were standing at the Red Sea, they began to doubt God's deliverance. Moses issued this strong word of exhortation, "And Moses said unto the people, Fear ye not, *stand still,* and see the salvation of the LORD, which he will show to you to day: for the Egyptians whom ye have seen to day, ye shall see them again no more for ever. The LORD shall fight for you, and ye shall hold your peace" (Exod. 14:13–14).

POWER OF OUR SWORD

Ephesians 6:17 says, "And take the helmet of salvation, and the sword of the Spirit, which is the word of God." What is your weapon against Satan's attack? The Word of God. "For the word of God is quick, and powerful, and sharper than any two-edged sword, piercing even to the dividing asunder of soul and spirit, and of the joints and marrow, and is a discerner of the thoughts and intents of the heart" (Heb. 4:12).

When faced with temptation, do you just open up the Bible and point to a verse? No. To fight, you must do much more than that. You need to study it and defend it. And more importantly, you need to *use* it—and use it *offensively.*

To know the critical importance of this, read Matthew 4:1–11. Notice that every time Satan tempted Jesus, he responded, "It is written." Jesus ran Satan through with this sharp sword when Satan tempted him in the wilderness. And Satan was impaled on that sword.

You can also use the sword to witness to the unsaved. The Word of God will cut to the quick. When Peter and the other apostles stood before the Sanhedrin to defend their faith, the members of this body were convicted: "When they heard that [the gospel], they were cut to the heart, and took counsel to slay them" (Acts 5:33).

PROVISION OF OUR SUPPLICATION

Finally, we must pray. Ephesians 6:18 says, "Praying always with all prayer and supplication in the Spirit, and watching thereunto with all perseverance and supplication for all saints." Our sword is the sword of the Spirit. Therefore, we are to pray in the Spirit—allowing the Holy Spirit to guide and empower our prayer.

Remember, the prayer that gets to heaven is the prayer that starts in heaven. We simply close the circuit. Through prayer the Holy Spirit wields his sword and brings it into the battle.

Paul says we are to wrestle in prayer (Rom. 15:30). While we are to be surefooted and stand, this does not mean there will not be a battle. The Greek word for wrestle is *sunagonizonai.* It means to "agonize together with." It's the word from which we get our word *agony*. There is a battle already won, but it is through prayer that is bold and persistent, anointed with the Holy Spirit, that victory is appropriated.

The Christian Warrior and His Allies

One final word about the battle: we must remember we're in this war together. Paul tells us, "And take the helmet of salvation, and the sword of the Spirit, which is the word of God: praying always with all prayer and supplication in the Spirit, and watching thereunto with all perseverance and supplication for *all saints; and for me,* that utterance may be given unto me, that I may open my mouth boldly, to make known the mystery of the gospel" (Eph. 6:17–19).

Paul knew that we are in the battle together. There is no such thing as "Lone Ranger" Christianity. We owe to one another a fearful loyalty. "Like a mighty army moves the church of God." Joshua 23:10 promises, "One man of you shall chase a thousand: for the LORD your God, he it is that fighteth for you, as he hath promised you." If one may chase a thousand, two should chase ten thousand like it talks about in Deuteronomy 32:30.

Let me suggest two things for you to do with reference to your brothers and sisters who are engaged in spiritual warfare with you.

First, pray fervently for them. Notice that the great apostle Paul, doubtless fully dressed in armor with the sword in his hand, still asked for prayer. We ought to soak our pastors and leaders in prayer. We should also intercede for all of those family members and comrades who join the battle with us.

Next, we should enlist others to pray for us. Sometimes tears come to my eyes when a friend tells me with sincerity that he or she is praying for me on a regular basis. What a comfort.

One last word. Check your armor now—not later, NOW! Are you fully dressed for the battle? Here is a true story from Bob Vernon with the Los Angeles Police Department:

The sun was just coming up. The motorcycle officer moved smoothly through the quiet Los Angeles suburb on his way in to work. As he neared an intersection, a red pickup truck sped past without even slowing for the stop sign. The officer turned on his flashing lights and radioed the station that he was in pursuit of the red vehicle.

As his unit pulled up behind the slowing truck, the officer was thinking, "This fellow is probably late for work." Unknown to the officer, the driver of the pickup had just robbed an all-night grocery store. On the seat beside the driver was the paper bag with the money and the gun he had used. The driver was thinking, "The cops know already." He was scared. He rested his hand on the gun.

The truck pulled to the side of the roadway and stopped. The officer parked his motorcycle and approached the driver's side of the pickup. He was relaxed, "Good morning sir. May I see your . . ." He didn't even get to finish his sentence. The driver stuck his arm out of the truck and fired his weapon. The barrel of the gun was only two inches away from the officer. The bullet hit the officer in the center of his chest. He was knocked to the ground seven feet away.

For a few moments, all was quiet. Then, to the horror of the gunman, the officer slowly stood to his feet. The driver couldn't believe it, "This guy must be Clark Kent." In shock, the policeman slowly began to brush the dirt from his uniform. After two or three seconds, the officer regained his wits, pulled his service revolver, and fired two rounds into the side of the truck. The first round went through the open window and destroyed the windshield. The second round went through the side of the door and ripped into the driver's left leg. "Don't shoot," screamed the terrified robber, throwing the gun and the bag of money out of the window.

The officer's life had been spared because he was wearing a bulletproof vest. Vests are incredibly strong even though they are only about three-eighths of an inch thick. They are made of dozens of layers of an extremely tough fabric called Kevlar.

A few months later another officer, Ray Hicks, and his partner went to serve a search warrant on a well-known drug dealer in the city of Inglewood. As his partner knocked, Hicks yelled out "Police!" and started to kick down the door. From inside the shabby apartment, four slugs were fired through the door. One found its mark. The impact was almost exactly where the motorcycle officer had been hit only a few weeks before—squarely in the center of the chest.

Later his partner recalled that Hicks said quietly, "I'm hit," and slowly sank to the floor. The coroner reported that the policeman probably lived less than a minute. The bullet had ruptured an artery; blood to the brain had been stopped instantly.

Police officer Ray Hicks was twenty-seven years old. He left a wife and three children. His bulletproof vest was found in the trunk of his car parked thirty feet from where he fell.

Every police officer in Los Angeles believes in bulletproof vests. They work! I doubt you could find a policeman anywhere who doesn't believe vests save lives.

But that is not enough. An officer must do more than believe in vests. He must take his belief to the point of personal commitment. He must be willing to wear the vest, and wear it at all times. Even when it is hot. Even when it is uncomfortable.

It is not enough just to believe that a man named Jesus lived two thousand years ago. We must take this belief to a point of commitment. We must be willing to take this belief to the point of "putting on" the risen Christ, receiving him as Savior and Lord.

The church is our battle station. We must never be AWOL. We should choose sides wisely, check our armor carefully, join the battle bravely, and enjoy the victory constantly.

PART II

Understanding the Principles of Kingdom Authority

CHAPTER 5

STRENGTH THROUGH SURRENDER

"The weakest saint can experience the power of the Deity of the Son of God if once he is willing to 'let go.' Any strand of our energy will blur the life of Jesus. We have to keep letting go, and slowly and surely the great full life of God will invade us in every part, and men will take knowledge of us that we have been with Jesus."
— OSWALD CHAMBERS

THE SECRET OF KINGDOM AUTHORITY

God does not give Kingdom Authority and all its potential to rebels. In fact, most of us have about all the authority with which God can trust us.

When we teach our teenagers to drive, where do we begin? The accelerator? The steering wheel? No, always with the brake! If you can't get your teen interested in the brake, then you aren't interested in showing him the accelerator. In the same way, you will never really know the *release* of the Spirit until you yield to the *restraint* of the Spirit. We must first master our spiritual brakes. We must learn that strength comes from surrendering.

I had the privilege to preach in Romania shortly after God brought spiritual revival to this nation that had been liberated from a cruel Communist government. One of the leaders in that revival was a man named Josef T'son. Part of what made this man a mighty servant of the Lord was his exercise of Kingdom Authority in his life. Suffering at the hands of the Communists with brutal beatings, imprisonments, and death threats, he learned the victory that comes so sweetly in surrendering to the Savior.

As Josef and I rode along in his car, I said, "Josef, tell me about American Christianity."

He said, "Adrian, I had rather not."

I said, "No, I want to know."

He then said, "Well, Adrian, since you have asked me, I'll tell you. The key word in American Christianity is *commitment*."

I said, "That is good, isn't it, Josef?"

He replied, "No, it is not. As a matter of fact, the word *commitment* did not come into great usage in the English language until about the 1960s. In Romania we do not even have a word to translate the English word *commitment*. If you were to use *commitment* in your message tonight, I would not have a proper word to translate it with."

Josef continued, "When a new word comes into usage, it generally pushes an old word out. I began to study and found the old word that *commitment* replaced. Adrian, the old word that is no longer in vogue in America is the word *surrender*."

"Josef," I asked, "What is the difference between *commitment* and *surrender?*"

He said, "When you make a commitment, you are still in control, no matter how noble the thing you commit to. One can commit to pray, to study the Bible, to give his money, or to commit to automobile payments, or to lose weight. Whatever he chooses to do, he *commits* to. But *surrender* is different. If someone holds a gun and asks you to lift your hands in the air as a token of surrender, you don't tell that person what you are committed to. You simply surrender and do as you are told."

He said, "Americans love commitment because they are still in control. But the key word is *surrender.* We are to be the slaves of the Lord Jesus Christ."

I had to say "Amen" in my heart. Never were more profound words spoken. And never a greater challenge given than those words to me that day. Of course, there are many things we may be committed to in a godly and wholesome way, but nothing can take the place of absolute surrender.

I did some more reflecting on this. In Titus 1:1, Paul says that he is a *doulos* of Jesus Christ. This word refers to a slave. It speaks of one who is in a permanent relationship of servitude to one whose will is swallowed up in the will of another. Specifically, it signified one who was born a bond slave in contrast to an *andrapodon*—one who was captured or sold into slavery.

In the New Testament, the word *doulos* is often translated by the word *servant,* which sounds a little softer. The New Testament uses this word to show the sinner's relationship to sin. Jesus said, "Whosoever committeth sin is the servant of sin" (John 8:34). After the bondage to sin has ended, however, *doulos* is then used to describe the believer's new relationship to God. Believers are not merely servants; they are devoted slaves of Jesus Christ.

Lest that story seem too austere, let us remind ourselves that we are talking about *strength through surrender.* To be strong is to admit you are personally weak. Then perfect freedom comes from absolute surrender. A story in the Word of God can also provide another illustration of this critical truth.

Luke records the story of a miraculous healing that took place in Capernaum (Luke 7:1–10). Not long after Jesus entered the city, some messengers approached him and told him that the beloved servant of a centurion was near death. Their message was very simple, "Will you heal this dying servant?"

Jesus headed for the officer's home, but before he arrived, he received another message from the centurion, "Lord, trouble not thyself: for I am not worthy that thou shouldest enter under my roof: wherefore neither thought I myself worthy to come unto thee: but say in a word, and my servant shall be healed. For *I also am a man set under authority,* having under me soldiers, and I say unto one, Go, and he goeth; and to another, Come, and he cometh; and to my servant, Do this, and he doeth it" (vv. 6–8).

At this point Jesus turned to those around him and remarked that this was the greatest faith he had found in all Israel. Not just *good* faith, but that he had "not found so great faith, no, not in Israel" (v. 9)! The Bible says Jesus "marveled" at what he heard. What was it that astounded the very Son of God? (By the way, if you cause Jesus to marvel, you have done an amazing thing.)

The key is found in Luke 7:8, where the centurion said, "For I also am a man set under authority." He was a man who understood the principle of Kingdom Authority. And that amazed and pleased the Savior.

The centurion's reputation as a proud and prominent military officer preceded him and gave him an immediate audience with Jesus. He had one hundred men serving under him in the most successful military unit in the history of the world. But this centurion's sterling reputation was the last thing on his mind when he sent messengers to intercept Jesus as he entered the city gates. He thought only of Jesus and of his beloved dying servant.

Yet when the centurion realized that Jesus was actually headed to his home, he quickly dispatched word that he, a high-ranking officer, was not worthy of a house call from this Jewish peasant! He told Jesus that one word from his lips was sufficient to heal his servant. "I, too," he reasoned, "am a man set under authority." That is, people reported to him because he reported to other people above him. That is the way the system worked and continues to work. The centurion knew he could not have soldiers as servants for protection and provision under him if he was not surrendered to the officers over him.

As clearly as I can, let me sum up again the whole matter of authority. When it comes to authority, *you cannot be over those things that God wants you to be over until you learn to be under those things that God has set over you.*

When the centurion said, "I also am a man set under authority," he was recognizing that Jesus in his humanity was operating on the same principle. Disease, death, and demons are subject to Jesus because he was subject to his Father.

This is the essence of Kingdom Authority. Fathers can have no authority in the home until they have surrendered to the headship of Jesus. Mothers cannot pray with authority for their children when they have no submissive spirit to their own husbands. Pastors cannot lead, teach, or preach with anointing and supernatural power without being fully broken and surrendered to the lordship of Christ, the authority of the Word, and the commands of the Spirit.

Do you know what *authority* means? The legal right to act. Eureka! Jesus' face lit up! Here was a man who knew the score! Jesus must have encountered thousands of people by this time in his travels across the country. And each time, he taught and ministered with the same authority. He had even tried to make his disciples understand; and finally here was a man—a Roman—who had a simple, yet powerful understanding of Jesus' spiritual authority.

Kingdom Authority is ultimately quite simple and quite powerful. It is simply this—you can never be *over* until you're *under.* Because Jesus, as a man, submitted himself to the Father; and the Father, in turn, committed himself to Jesus. Jesus was *over* all because he was totally *under* the Father and had been given authority.

Two passages from God's Word teach us this principle of Christ's submission and his resulting power:

> And what is the exceeding greatness of his power to us-ward who believe, according to the working of his mighty power, which he wrought in Christ, when he raised him from the dead, and set him at his own right hand in the heavenly

places, far above all principality, and power, and might, and dominion, and every name that is named, not only in this world, but also in that which is to come: and hath put all things under his feet, and gave him to be the head over all things to the church, which is his body, the fulness of him that filleth all in all (Eph. 1:19–23).

For by him were all things created, that are in heaven, and that are in earth, visible and invisible, whether they be thrones, or dominions, or principalities, or powers: all things were created by him, and for him: and he is before all things, and by him all things consist. And he is the head of the body, the church: who is the beginning, the firstborn from the dead; that in all things he might have the preeminence. For it pleased the Father that in him should all fulness dwell (Col. 1:16–19).

THE SOURCE OF KINGDOM AUTHORITY

All human authority descends from a higher power above. No one has authority without being under authority. The centurion did not let his power go to his head. He understood the things above him as well as the things below him.

How long would the centurion's power over his underlings last if those above him did not back him up? If he rebelled against the authority above him, not only would his authority be taken away, but he might be put into prison or even executed.

We must remember that our authority comes from above. In John 5:16–46, our Lord's response to the Pharisees turns on this same principle. Jesus had healed a man on the Sabbath. When the Pharisees heard about it, they became incensed. They were already upset with Jesus because he claimed that God was his Father. What was Jesus' response to their impassioned rage? Jesus responded, "Verily, verily, I say unto you, The Son can do nothing of himself, but what he seeth the Father do: for what things soever he doeth, these also doeth the Son likewise. For the Father loveth the Son, and showeth him all things that himself

doeth: and he will show him greater works than these, that ye may marvel" (vv. 19–20).

Jesus Christ in his humanity saw himself as a channel for the
Father's power and the Father's Word; and, therefore, exercised great
power and authority. He claimed no word, no authority, and no power
of his own as man but only that which came from the perfect depend-
ence upon God's provision and will.

The strength of Kingdom Authority is incredible. We do not have to
possess physical, intellectual, financial, or political strength to overcome
Satan. All we need is God-given authority through Jesus.

When Jesus commissioned the seventy to go out and preach, he sent
them out with power and authority. And they returned with the glow of
victory on their faces: "And the seventy returned again with joy, saying,
Lord, even the devils are subject unto us *through thy name.* And he said
unto them, I beheld Satan as lightning fall from heaven. Behold, I give
unto you power to tread on serpents and scorpions, and over all the
power of the enemy: and nothing shall by any means hurt you"
(Luke 10:17–19).

When a police officer asks you to open the door "in the name of the
law," he is appealing to the law of the land. The person on the other side
of the door knows that the local forces of law enforcement will back up
what the officer is asking, otherwise no one would have to open the
door. When you pray, "in the name of Jesus," you appeal to Lord of the
law. God the Father will act on behalf of the name of Jesus or else our
prayers would be a waste of time.

A 275-pound defensive tackle exhibits brute force that can be intimidating to most people on or off a playing field. But you know what? A
little man in a striped shirt half his size can blow a whistle and order him
off the field. The striped shirt signals his authority, and the football
player must recognize it and obey it, or he isn't allowed in the game.

Jesus has given you a striped shirt and a whistle. You have Kingdom
Authority over the power of that terrible creature who bedevils the
earth. It is time that you and I whistle him off the field!

THE CHALLENGE OF KINGDOM AUTHORITY

Before we can have the victory of Kingdom Authority, we must first surrender to the King of authority. Satan isn't going to stop laughing and mocking at our attempts to exercise authority when we ourselves have not lifted our hands in surrender to the Almighty. We must surrender all things to his glory. And that includes everything from our bank accounts, to our business dealings, to our educational curriculum, and our social justice system.

In the chapters that follow we will be thinking about those things that God has set over us. If we are wise, we will place ourselves *under* his authority so we can be *over* Satan's power and deceptive schemes. We cannot have his authority until we submit to his lordship. We must abandon our rebellious ways and learn the liberation of surrender to the King of kings!

Remember again the principle: We will never be over those things that God has set under us until we learn to be under those things that God has placed over us. There is strength through surrender.

Are you under the Word of God? Is the Bible your mandate for life? Are you loving it, reading it, obeying it, and living it? Are you consciously filled with the Holy Spirit? Have you yielded every part of the temple of your body to him? Are you grieving him in any way?

Are you graciously submitting to those human authorities that God has set over you: in the home, in the church, in civil government, and in the workplace? Have you made Jesus Christ the absolute Lord over *everything* in your life?

Charles Haddon Spurgeon gave a challenge over one hundred years ago that still rings true today:

> Lose all rather than lose your integrity, and when all else is gone, still hold fast a clear conscience as the rarest jewel which can adorn the bosom of a mortal. Be not guided by the will-o-the-wisp of policy, but by the pole star of *divine authority*. Follow the right at all hazards. When you see no present advantage, walk by faith and not by sight. Do God the honour

to trust Him when it comes to matters of loss for the sake of principle. See whether He will be your debtor! See if He doth not even in this life prove His word that "Godliness, with contentment, is great gain," and that they who "seek first the kingdom of God and His righteousness, shall have all these things added unto them."

When you are willing to be to Jesus what Jesus was in his humanity to the Father, then Jesus will be to your humanity what the Father was to him. Paul tells us we are to have the same attitude as that of our Lord:

> Let this mind be in you, which was also in Christ Jesus: who, being in the form of God, thought it not robbery to be equal with God: but made himself of no reputation, and took upon him the form of a servant, and was made in the likeness of men: and being found in fashion as a man, he humbled himself, and became obedient unto death, even the death of the cross. Wherefore God also hath highly exalted him, and given him a name which is above every name: that at the name of Jesus every knee should bow, of things in heaven, and things in earth, and things under the earth; and that every tongue should confess that Jesus Christ is Lord, to the glory of God the Father (Phil. 2:5–11).

Before you go to the next chapter, take a moment and lift both hands in absolute surrender to his majesty . . . his throne of grace and mercy. King Jesus is worthy. And don't be afraid to do it. The attempt to save your life will only cause you to lose it (Mark 8:35). A wise man said, "The slave to the compass has freedom of the seas. The rest must sail close to the shore."

CHAPTER 6

LIMITS OF OUR KINGDOM AUTHORITY

No man can look with undivided vision at God and at the world of reality so long as God and the world are torn asunder. Try as he may, he can only let his eyes wander distractedly from one to the other. But there is a place at which God and the cosmic reality are reconciled, a place at which God and man have become one. That and that alone is what enables man to set his eyes upon God and the world at the same time. This place does not lie somewhere out beyond reality in the realm of ideas. It lies in the midst of history as a divine miracle. It lies in Jesus Christ, the reconciler of the world.
—DIETRICH BONHOEFFER

There are some well-meaning believers in the body of Christ who believe that salvation is the elimination of all pain and suffering. I hate to disappoint them, but life is not "all honey and no bees," whether you are saved or lost.

Kingdom Authority is not the key to Fort Knox and the fountain of youth rolled into one. It is not the gospel of cash, fancy cars, yachts, and vacation homes as promised by the "joy boys" on television. The truth of spiritual authority has been distorted and often discarded because of this dominion theology gospel saying that you can simply "name it and claim it" as part of your authority as a believer. "Just call on the Lord, and you can have it all."

Can we, with Kingdom Authority, speak our way to prosperity and great riches? Can we curse cancer and cause it to wither away? Can we, at will, defy and subdue wild animals? These are questions we must answer to fully comprehend the limits and privileges of Kingdom Authority.

SPIRITUAL AUTHORITY

Kingdom Authority is a glorious truth not to be refused, confused, or abused. It is a powerful responsibility given to us by God himself when we became his children. I say this reverently because this is a critical point we need to grasp before we go any further. I need to define the difference between authority in the spiritual and physical realms.

Before sin cursed the natural world, man had authority over *all* created things. Adam's dominion was over the beasts of the field, the fowls of the air, and the fish of the sea, according to Genesis 1:28 and Psalm 8:6–8. But when God cast Adam and Eve out of the Garden of Eden (Gen. 3:23–24), that authority was lost.

Today, Christians have been given *spiritual authority* over the world, the flesh, and the devil. God has not now given us authority over things in the material or natural world, like microbes, mosquitoes, mildew, or mudslides. These are a part of this natural world and the curse that comes with it. If you throw a rock into a hornet's nest, you just might get stung! The Spirit-filled life is not a guarantee of protection from the physical curses of the natural world.

THERE IS A "NOT YET"

Though our authority is limited now, one day it will be fully restored. One day our bodies will be redeemed. Then we will have authority over the material universe of disease, disaster, and death.

Hebrews 2:6–8 says, "What is man, that thou art mindful of him? or the son of man, that thou visitest him? Thou madest him a little lower than the angels; thou crownedst him with glory and honour, and didst set him over the works of thy hands: thou hast put all things in subjection under his feet. For in that he put all in subjection under him, he left nothing that is not put under him. But now we see *not yet all things put under him.*" The key phrase in this passage is "not yet." There is a "not yet" to be reckoned with because the curse of sin is still on the natural world.

The Kingdom Authority that we have in this age is *spiritual* authority. We are not pawns in a cosmic game of chess. We have God's Spirit living within us. Through redemption God has given us all things that pertain to life and godliness. Second Peter 1:3 says, "According as his divine power hath given unto us all things that pertain unto life and godliness, through the knowledge of him that hath called us to glory and virtue." Potentially, we gain far more in Christ than we ever lost in Adam; but we are waiting for the full inheritance when Jesus comes again.

THERE IS A BETTER DAY COMING

God said Adam and Eve would die the very day they sinned. And yet strangely the Scripture records that they lived for many centuries and had sons and daughters. It this a contradiction? Not at all. Remember that man is body, soul, and spirit. Let me tell you how Adam died as a result of his sin.

- **He died immediately in his spirit.** The Lord of life moved out of Adam, and now he was dead in his trespasses and sin. Death is not primarily the separation of the soul from the body, but the spirit from God.
- **He died progressively in his soul.** His mind now had become a garden of weeds. Among his first uttered words after the transgression were these, "I was afraid." Shame, fear, negativism, and neuroses filled his mind. God, to him now, was no

longer someone to walk with but someone to hide from. Now God has to chase us to save us.

- **He died ultimately in his body.** Adam's body, with the seed of death in it, existed for 930 years, but there is a sense in which it was already dead. Adam was very much like a Christmas tree cut off from its roots, brought into the house and decorated. In some ways, it may look better in the house than it did out in the wild. But what happened when it was cut from the source of life will show some time after New Year's. The truth of the matter is, that it is often called a living tree, but it was dead when it was cut off from the source of life. So it is with man.

Keep this in mind when you consider what God has done for us and will do in salvation. When you were born from above, Almighty God began a reverse process in your life.

1. Whereas Adam died immediately in his spirit, you were instantaneously justified in the Spirit. In Jesus, "ye are washed, but ye are sanctified, but ye are justified in the name of the Lord Jesus, and by the Spirit of our God" (1 Cor. 6:11). Our Lord paid the price for your righteousness in full.

Romans 3:24 says, "Being justified freely by his grace through the redemption that is in Christ Jesus." And Romans 4:5, 8 promise, "But to him that worketh not, but believeth on him that justifieth the ungodly, his faith is counted for righteousness. . . . Blessed is the man to whom the Lord will not impute sin." Note that not only are our iniquities forgiven and our sins covered, but that the Scripture says God will not impute sin to us. What an incredible promise!

If God were to put one-half of one sin on our account, we would be eternally lost. I try to live a Christian life, but I will not trust the best fifteen minutes I ever lived to get me to heaven much less some of my bad ones. We're saved by grace and kept by grace.

2. Next, remember that whereas Adam died progressively in his soul, you are progressively sanctified in the soul. John 17:17 says, "Sanctify them through thy truth: thy word is truth." Philippians 2:12–13 says, "Work out your own salvation with fear and trembling. For it is God which worketh in you both to will and to do of his good pleasure." God is working in you throughout your life to present you faultless and perfect before his throne (Jude 24). Day by day we should grow in Christlikeness.

3. **Joyfully, this process culminates when we are ultimately glorified in the body—called the redemption of the body.** This third stage is what we're waiting for, it is the "not yet" part: "For we know that the whole creation groaneth and travaileth in pain together until now. And not only they, but ourselves also, which have the firstfruits of the Spirit, even we ourselves groan within ourselves, waiting for the adoption, to wit, the redemption of our body" (Rom. 8:22–23).

When you were born again, you became a child of God and received from God his nature. Along with this, you also needed legal standing with the Father. This legal standing is called "the adoption." A part of that adoption is the redemption of the body.

In Bible times if a man had a son by a slave and wanted this son to legally inherit his estate, there had to be a legal adoption ceremony. During this ceremony, the child was not only ingrafted into the family tree but was also presented with the *future* promise of his father's estate (an adopted son was not given the full inheritance as a child because he could not handle it; that would come later).

The Word of God teaches that not only do we have the indwelling Spirit by our new birth, but we also have the legal rights and riches of a son by adoption (see Eph. 1:3–11). This "spirit of adoption" is our present possession and the pledge of the future inheritance to come. *There is much more coming!*

Our full inheritance is the redemption of the body and all that comes with this redemption. Until that time we live in a world saturated with sickness, war, hate, riots, and confusion. Without proper perspective, we could easily become confused and discouraged and wonder if we have any authority at all. But we are not helpless. Although the trinity of evil—the world, the flesh, and the devil—wages war against us personally, it has no real legal power over us in this present age. Yes, we are limited in our power over the material universe now, but one day Christ will return, and we will reign with him! We will receive the full legacy.

Here are three vital truths in Romans 8 that we need to make sense of the sufferings we see in this present world.

Truth #1: Yesterday's Curse Brings Bondage

"For I reckon that the sufferings of this present time are not worthy to be compared with the glory which shall be revealed in us. For the earnest expectation of the creature waiteth for the manifestation of the sons of God. For the creature was made subject to vanity, not willingly, but by reason of him who hath subjected the same in hope, because the creature itself also shall be delivered from the bondage of corruption into the glorious liberty of the children of God. For we know that the whole creation groaneth and travaileth in pain together until now" (Rom. 8:18–22).

When Adam and Eve sinned, they dragged all of creation down with them. The world fell into what the Bible calls "the bondage of corruption" (Rom. 8:21). Now something is wrong. Confusion, frustration, and suffering rest upon all that God created on this planet.

Perhaps you've wondered, "How could a good God allow such bad things to happen?" Indeed, this question has caused some people to lose their faith. Once a person asks this question, there is a progression of thoughts: "God is the author of all things. Evil is some *thing*. Therefore, God is the author of evil."

This little syllogism, however, does not reflect things as they are. *God did not create evil.* God created a perfect world and said, "It is good." In his sovereign wisdom, God created man perfectly free because he wants our love and worship *above all else.* Forced love and forced worship is not love or worship at all. Man had to have the ability to choose evil in order to have the freedom to choose good.

When man chose evil of his own will, God put a curse upon creation. This curse was not only *for* judgment but also *in* mercy. The worst thing that could happen to fallen humanity would be to live with the infection of sin without the corresponding fever pain of corruption and bondage in the material world. Sinners in paradise would never repent. In the natural world the fever (sorrow) is there to let us know that there is a deeper infection (sin) that needs to be dealt with.

That brings another question, "Why doesn't God just kill the devil and destroy evil?" *God cannot destroy evil without destroying freedom (the ability to choose).* To destroy freedom would destroy the opportunity to love. And to destroy love would destroy the highest good. God does not, therefore, destroy evil. Rather, he *defeats* it.

Remember that dominion was legally lost and must be legally reclaimed. God is wisely and systematically doing just that. For now we must live with the bondage of corruption.

The animal kingdom is corrupted (Gen. 3:14). What some call the "survival of the fittest" is really creation groaning under the curse. Animals originally created to coexist in harmony are now mercilessly clawing their way to the top of the animal kingdom.

The mineral kingdom is corrupted (Gen. 3:17). Deserts, erosion, and wastelands scar the once beautiful face of God's green earth. Skies and oceans are polluted with man's industrial workmanship. Concrete highways ribbon the land where rivers and meadows once flourished.

The vegetable kingdom is corrupted (Gen. 3:18). The world has become a garden of weeds. The sweat of our brows waters the dandelions that have infiltrated our lawns and our rose gardens. And pests have set up camptown meetings in our vegetable patches.

Though we may be redeemed, we are not yet rescued. We must still live on planet Earth. We must still live in bodies while awaiting our glorified redemption when Christ returns. The human race has been spiritually dethroned, morally depraved, emotionally disturbed, and physically diseased. All of the sons and daughters of Adam have a polluted gene pool and are infected with a terminal illness. Death runs in our family.

We need to understand, therefore, that being saved does not make us immune to physical sufferings. Romans 8:23 teaches that we are a part of a ruined creation and that spiritual redemption does not automatically bring immunity from pain and suffering. Thank God that sometimes he chooses to heal according to his sovereign will, but not always. Our desire is that his will is done in all things even if suffering may be a part of it.

TRUTH #2: TOMORROW'S CONQUEST WILL BRING LIBERTY

"Because the creature itself also shall be delivered from the bondage of corruption into the glorious liberty of the children of God. For we know that the whole creation groaneth and travaileth in pain together until now. And not only they, but ourselves also, which have the firstfruits of the Spirit, even we ourselves groan within ourselves, waiting for the adoption, to wit, the redemption of our body" (Rom. 8:21–23).

Creation is pressed down with grief and distress. To try to save this world with a better system of ecology and social action is like rearranging the deck chairs on the *Titanic*. We need to do all we can do to take care of our bodies and to take care of our environment, but we are fighting a losing battle.

The golden age will dawn when Jesus returns. Meanwhile, all of nature is waiting and yearning with outstretched arms. When our Lord steps on the scene, the hills will skip like lambs, and the trees will clap their hands in joy. What a change there will be!

The animal kingdom will be changed. "The wolf will dwell with the lamb, and the lamb will not be inside the wolf" (Isa. 11:6–9). Whatever is evil in the animal kingdom will be glorious when Jesus returns. As will be seen in the rest of creation, animals will no longer be under the curse of disease. Their bodies will be strong and will be restored to the manner in which they were created. Perfect and complete—living in harmony, one with the other.

The mineral and vegetable kingdoms will be changed. The beauty of God's earth and its fruits will be resplendent in his glory. My wife Joyce and I experienced a taste of the hope of this transformation in a place called Butchart Gardens on Vancouver Island, British Columbia.

In the early 1900s, Robert Pim Butchart became a highly successful pioneer in the burgeoning industry of cement production. He built a factory at Tod Inlet on Vancouver Island and moved his family there. When he had exhausted the lime from the quarry, there was nothing left but a huge hole in the ground. His wife caught a vision and began an enterprising venture to transform the unsightly barren quarry into a thing of natural beauty. As the tourists began to flock in droves to their home, they renamed their estate "Benvenuto," the Italian word for "Welcome." Almost one hundred years later the wonderment of God's creation is evident among the more than one million bedding plants in over seventy varieties planted throughout the fifty-acre estate. Now you might comprehend a little of what will happen to the Sahara Desert in the age to come (Isa. 35:1).

Our bodies will be changed. The great news for us is the coming redemption of our bodies. Philippians 3:20–21 says, "For our conversation is in heaven; from whence also we look for the Saviour, the Lord Jesus Christ: who shall change our vile body, that it may be fashioned like unto his glorious body, according to the working whereby he is able even to subdue all things unto himself."

Think of your glorified body. You will be like him. Every vestige of sin will be removed. You will have ageless vitality. There will be no sorrow, trouble, weakness, or pain. Every wrinkle, blemish, and fault placed by the curse of sin will be erased forever, and in their place will be the likeness of Jesus Christ (see 1 John 3:2). It is then that we will shout with a loud "Amen!" to what Paul had prophesied: "For I reckon that the sufferings of this present time are not worthy to be compared with the glory which shall be revealed in us" (Rom. 8:18).

What a day that will be when he turns every tear to a pearl, every hurt to a hallelujah, and Calvary becomes your personal Easter!

TRUTH #3: TODAY'S COMFORT IS HOPE

"For we are saved by hope: but hope that is seen is not hope: for what a man seeth, why doth he yet hope for" (Rom. 8:24).

Remember that the groans we endure today are temporary. They are transfigured by a hope that is rock-solid certainty based on the promises of God.

There is the groaning of creation. "For the earnest expectation of the creature waiteth for the manifestation of the sons of God. For the creature was made subject to vanity, not willingly, but by reason of him who hath subjected the same in hope, because the creature itself also shall be delivered from the bondage of corruption into the glorious liberty of the children of God. For we know that the *whole creation groaneth* and travaileth in pain together until now" (Rom. 8:19–22).

Creation is groaning until Christ's return. This passage tells us that the "creature was made subject to vanity." Vanity means that it does not measure up to the original intention, but there is a better time coming for creation.

There is the groaning of the Christian. "And not only they, but ourselves also, which have the firstfruits of the Spirit, even we *ourselves groan within ourselves,* waiting for the adoption, to wit, the redemption of our body. For we are saved by hope: but hope that is seen is not hope: for what a man seeth, why doth he yet hope for? But if we hope for that we see not, then do we with patience wait for it" (Rom. 8:23–25).

Remember that as Christians we groan because we are part of this creation, but our groaning is transfigured by hope. The word *hope* in the Bible does not mean a weak "perhaps," but a *certain* and *glad* expectancy! The Christian's hope is wrapped up in the sure promise of the Second Coming of our great God and Savior Jesus. It is called the "blessed hope" (Titus 2:13). The suffering that we have now is just the black velvet upon which the diamond of God's glory will be revealed.

And there is the groaning of the Comforter. "Likewise the Spirit also helpeth our infirmities: for we know not what we should pray for as we ought: but the *Spirit itself maketh intercession for us with groanings which cannot be uttered.* And he that searcheth the hearts knoweth what is the mind of the Spirit, because he maketh intercession for the saints according to the will of God" (Rom. 8:26–27).

We don't have to bear these groanings alone. Jesus promised the Holy Spirit would come to be our Comforter (John 15:16). The Greek word for Comforter is *paraklētos,* which means an advocate. It comes from another word that means "to come alongside." The groanings that we endure are temporary, but the glory we expect is eternal. "For I reckon that the sufferings of this present time are not worthy to be compared with the glory which shall be revealed in us" (Rom. 8:18).

I have a beloved brother in Christ who is suffering from cancer. I have been encouraging him and praying with him. One day, he sent me a list of things that cancer cannot do.

- It cannot cripple love.
- It cannot shatter hope.
- It cannot corrode faith.
- It cannot eat away peace.
- It cannot destroy confidence.
- It cannot kill friendship.
- It cannot shut out memories.
- It cannot silence courage.
- It cannot invade the soul.
- It cannot reduce eternal life.
- It cannot quench the spirit.
- It cannot lessen the power of the resurrection.

No disease can rob you of God's presence. No illness can steal away his joy. No accident can dim his love for you. In Jesus we have the victory!

We are being prepared for glory. Rather than defeating us, all the curses of this world can draw the believing heart closer to the Lord. In these things we are more than conquerors—we are *super*-conquerors. In the midst of all of these things—the world, the flesh and the devil— we can experience the conquest of Kingdom Authority. They have no power over us.

HOPE FOR YOU

Romans 8 begins with *no condemnation,* and it ends with *no separation.* Remember that the love that lifted us from the miry clay will one day lift us to our ultimate authority where we will reign with Jesus. *There is more to come.* "But there is a place where someone has testified: 'What is man that you are mindful of him, the son of man that you care for him? You made him a little lower than the angels; you crowned him with glory and honor and put everything under his feet.' In putting everything under him, God left nothing that is not subject to him. Yet at present we do not see everything subject to him" (Heb. 2:6–8 NIV).

One day all things will be under our feet! What a day that will be . . . *but not yet!* For now, we see in a mirror dimly, but one day we will see him face-to-face (1 Cor. 13:12). In a book entitled *Count It All Joy,* Barbara Lee Johnson had this to say about that day when we will see Jesus:

> How sad it will be to stand before the Lord one day and see what we might have become, what riches and glory we might have shared, what power and love we might have possessed; all opportunities that slipped away by our refusal to see God in our circumstances!
>
> It will be cause of great lament to realize we dragged our feet through our problems when we might have flown over them on the wings of an eagle of trust. To be discouraged, downhearted, distressed, or disappointed when we might have had "joy unspeakable and full of glory" (1 Pet. 1:8)—what a tragic thought![1]

I want you to fly on the wings of Kingdom Authority. I want you to know the power and peace that comes from knowing the God who loves you and has given you authority to be victorious in all things. My prayer for you comes from Paul's letter to the Ephesians. Though chained to a prison cell, his heart soared on the wings of the Lord. I pray that you would grasp the hope of your calling in Christ and the powerful love he has given you.

That the God of our Lord Jesus Christ, the Father of glory, may give unto you the spirit of wisdom and revelation in the knowledge of him: the eyes of your understanding being enlightened; that ye may know what is the hope of his calling, and what the riches of the glory of his inheritance in the saints, and what is the exceeding greatness of his power to us-ward who believe, according to the working of his mighty power, which he wrought in Christ, when he raised him from the dead, and set him at his own right hand in the heavenly places, far above all principality, and power, and might, and dominion, and every name that is named, not only in this world, but also in that which is to come: and hath put all things under his feet, and gave him to be the head over all things to the church, which is his body, the fulness of him that filleth all in all (Eph. 1:17–23).

While we wait for the full release of our legacy, remember that day-by-day we may now exercise Kingdom Authority over the world, the flesh, and the devil and live as super-conquerors.

CHAPTER 7

THE PROBLEM OF UNWORTHY AUTHORITIES

GODLESS GOVERNMENTS, BAD BOSSES, AND MEAN MATES

God establishes earthly authorities, but God does not give Kingdom Authority to rebels. As we have repeatedly discovered, we can never be *over those things* God has put *under* us until we are *under those things* that he has set *over* us. All of us live under authority that God has set over us.

God gives Kingdom Authority to his children who have a *spirit of submission*—even when those authorities over them are not worthy of submission. As children of God, it is our responsibility to submit to the authorities of government, work, and the home.

This will seem well and good until we have to submit to what we believe is an unworthy authority. Has this ever happened to you? Sometimes we are left with godless governments, bad bosses, and mean mates. The world is full of them, so how can we submit? What if we are commanded to do something wrong?

Let's look at one example. If a wife is to submit to her husband because he is God's authoritative head in the home, does this include submission to an abusive husband? Here's a letter I received that illustrates this question:

Dear Dr. Rogers,

After today's sermon I felt compelled to write this letter. You spoke of submitting to authorities, even evil ones that don't deserve respect. I do agree with this, but my heart just hurts for people who are in abusive situations as I was and take statements like that as reasons to stay in abusive marriages.

I am married to a man who has been abusive to me mentally, physically, verbally, and sexually. I was never "battered" physically, so to speak, but was slapped, pushed, etc., on several (fourteen) occasions over a six-year period. I stayed because I felt that was what God intended for me and because I never heard anything other than "wives submit to your husbands" even when they don't deserve it. My husband was a professing Christian, and he would often use the Bible to "beat me over the head." (Not literally, of course.)

After six years, the last two really being the worst, my coping skills were beginning to erode. The day after an episode of physical, verbal, and sexual abuse I prayed, "Lord, I'm at my end. I have always felt you wanted me to fulfill my vows to you to stay in this marriage. But now I truly want to do your will. If it is to stay, I will stay, relying on your grace and strength. If it is to leave, I will leave relying on your courage and wisdom."

Does this sound familiar? "Every nine seconds a woman or a child in this country is battered or abused at home. Each year more than six thousand women and children die from abuse. Domestic violence is the leading cause of injury to women ages 15–44—more common than automobile accidents, mugging, or rapes."[1]

Later I will share with you what she did. For now, I think this letter is a classic example of a genuine problem. Do we submit to evil people who are in control? in work? school? government? The problem is not a new one. Peter in his letter to suffering Christians in the first century faced the same kind of issues.

Tough times have arrived. It was "open season" on the early Christians, and it's "open season" on us today. First-century believers were accused of any imaginary charge the Roman government could create: incest (for calling wives or husbands "brother" and "sister"); cannibalism (partaking of the body and blood of Christ); insurrection (Jesus was Lord, not Caesar). These alleged incestuous men and women, cannibals, and insurrectionists became Rome's "Most Wanted." They were hounded, hunted, and killed.

Jesus said, "If the world hate you, ye know that it hated me before it hated you" (John 15:18). He was falsely accused as a wine lover, glutton, and insurrectionist. But he taught the principle of submission. Shouldn't overcomers be rebels? No! We practice a higher principle that closes the mouths of our accusers. We are to submit. Peter, in the following passage, mentions three areas of submission to unworthy authorities:

> Dearly beloved, I beseech you as strangers and pilgrims, abstain from fleshly lusts, which war against the soul; having your conversation honest among the Gentiles: that, whereas they speak against you as evildoers, they may by your good works, which they shall behold, glorify God in the day of visitation.
>
> Submit yourselves to every ordinance of man for the Lord's sake: whether it be to the king, as supreme; or unto governors, as unto them that are sent by him for the punishment of evildoers, and for the praise of them that do well.
>
> For so is the will of God, that with well doing ye may put to silence the ignorance of foolish men: as free, and not using your liberty for a cloak of maliciousness, but as the servants of

God. Honour all men. Love the brotherhood. Fear God.
Honour the king.

Servants, be subject to your masters with all fear; not only
to the good and gentle, but also to the froward. For this is
thankworthy, if a man for conscience toward God endure grief,
suffering wrongfully (1 Pet. 2:11–19).

Likewise, ye wives, be in subjection to your own husbands;
that, if any obey not the word, they also may without the word
be won by the conversation of the wives (1 Pet. 3:1).

Notice that Peter hammers this point home. Submission applies to
every context and at every level. To the government, he tells us to "honour the king" (1 Pet. 2:17). In our work, he tells us to "be subject to your
masters with all fear" (1 Pet. 2:18). In the home, wives are to "be in subjection" to their husbands (1 Pet. 3:1).

First Peter 2:15 says, "For so is the will of God, that with well doing
ye may put to *silence* the ignorance of foolish men." The Greek word
phimoō for "silence" means to muzzle as we would muzzle an annoying
dog who barks in the night.

Peter teaches that all we can do is act in a way that first makes their
jaws drop—then shuts their mouths. Without saying a word, they should
recognize something in us that is not of this earth. Those opposing the
ways of God can only be described as ignorant and foolish. We silence
them not with sedition, but submission.

In some cases, however, we must speak out against them, and sometimes even refuse to obey, if those authorities violate God's law. The
saint needs to be very careful when he or she does this, however.

THE PRINCIPLE OF SUBMISSION

When we are left with godless governments, bad bosses, and mean
mates, do we simply give in? What if we are asked to do something
wrong?

Kingdom Authority works in a unique way—we will never be *over*
until we're *under*. First Peter 2:13a says, "Submit yourselves to every

ordinance of man *for the Lord's sake."* The principle of submission is simply this: one person voluntarily placing himself under another person *for God's glory.* It is not for the sake of the authority we recognize, but for the sake of God who established the authority. And this makes all the difference in the world.

Remember, God has set all authorities in place. Romans 13:1–7 says:

> Let every soul be subject unto the higher powers. For there is no power but of God: the powers that be are ordained of God. Whosoever therefore resisteth the power, resisteth the ordinance of God: and they that resist shall receive to themselves damnation.
>
> For rulers are not a terror to good works, but to the evil. Wilt thou then not be afraid of the power? do that which is good, and thou shalt have praise of the same: for he is the minister of God to thee for good. But if thou do that which is evil, be afraid; for he beareth not the sword in vain: for he is the minister of God, a revenger to execute wrath upon him that doeth evil.
>
> Wherefore ye must needs be subject, not only for wrath, but also for conscience sake. For for this cause pay ye tribute also: for they are God's ministers, attending continually upon this very thing. Render therefore to all their dues: tribute to whom tribute is due; custom to whom custom; fear to whom fear; honour to whom honour.

When we submit to a godless government, a bad boss, or a mean mate, we are really submitting to God; he honors that and invests in us Kingdom Authority. To submit is to imitate Jesus who humbled himself and became obedient unto death. You may recall how Philippians 2:6–8 exhorts us with the submission of Christ, "Who, being in the form of God, thought it not robbery to be equal with God: but made himself of no reputation, and took upon him the form of a servant, and was made in the likeness of men: and being found in fashion as a man, he humbled himself, and became obedient unto death, even the death of the cross."

If we rebel, on the other hand, it is in the spirit of the ultimate rebel: Satan. And rebellion is what made the devil what he is today. It is also related to witchcraft (see 1 Sam. 15:23). What happens when we rebel? The same that happened to the devil. When Satan tried to reposition himself upward, God sent him to the bottom.

When Jesus humbled himself, God lifted him up, "Wherefore God also hath highly exalted him, and given him a name which is above every name . . . and that every tongue should confess that Jesus Christ is Lord, to the glory of God the Father" (Phil. 2:9–11). The secret of Jesus' authority is the principle of submission.

THE PLACES OF SUBMISSION

1. Submission to Godless Government. The first place Peter urges us to submit is to the government (1 Pet. 2:13–14, 17): "Submit yourselves to every ordinance of man for the Lord's sake: whether it be to the king, as supreme; or unto governors, as unto them that are sent by him for the punishment of evildoers, and for the praise of them that do well. . . . Honour all men. Love the brotherhood. Fear God. Honour the king."

That's fine for godly kings, but what about an ungodly king? Well, who do you think was the emperor in Peter's day? Nero! Nero was three years old when his father, a "killer, a bully, and a cheat" (according to one source) died. His mother then murdered his stepfather with poison mushrooms.

Nero learned some gruesome things when he was a child. It's no wonder that he became a teenage murderer himself. At fifteen, he had his own wife killed, then later his second wife. He murdered the husband of his third wife, then his own mother. He survived a death sentence, as well as his own attempted suicide by cutting his throat at age thirty-one. Does this sound like a ruler to whom you want to submit? But Peter commanded his followers to honor this king—and all kings— *for the Lord's sake.*

Let me say some government is *always* necessary. C. S. Lewis said that "democracy is given not that we are all equally intelligent or equally moral; the point is that we are equally sinful. Therefore authority is necessary; we need to keep an eye on one another."

But even a totalitarian government is better than anarchy and mob rule.

We are to honor the king. It doesn't matter whether he is president, king, czar, or prime minister. I must confess that I find this command extremely difficult after some of the escapades that took place in America's highest office in a former administration. I have had to bite my tongue and also ask forgiveness on some occasions. I do not honor immorality and lying, but I must honor authority. The civil authorities are ordained by God (see Rom. 13:1).

Can you submit to godless authorities? Not on your own. This kind of living takes supernatural power.

I've already mentioned my friend Josef T'son earlier in this book. He was hated by the Romanian secret police who operated under a cruel Communist regime. One day, they came to Josef's house to search his library for any books, sermons, or material that would be considered contraband.

Josef told me that it was a sad day for him to watch these ruthless men rummage through his personal things, to package up his books (a preacher's tool in trade), and cart them away. They were making him sign every book in case something was found there that could be used against him. He was feeling miserable when one of the soldiers handed him a book to sign, entitled *Joy Unspeakable and Full of Glory: Are You Experiencing It Now?* Josef knew that it was God's message. It spoke joy to his heart. He said, "I chose to rejoice in spite of these circumstances." He called out to his wife, "Elizabeth, we have guests in our house. Fix some coffee for them." From that time on, Josef said he was no longer being beaten down. To the contrary, he was ruling like a king.

2. Submission to Bad Bosses. First Peter 2:18–19 exhort servants to "be subject to your masters with all fear; not only to the good and gentle, but also to the froward. For this is thankworthy, if a man for conscience toward God endure grief, suffering wrongfully." The Greek word *oiketēs* for "servant" refers to a household servant.

In those days, servants were treated as possessions. They were not seen as persons but things. Aristotle's philosophy had come to full flower: "Master and slave have nothing in common; a slave is a living tool, just as a tool is an inanimate slave." It was the dynamite of the gospel that would ultimately bring down the house of slavery.

Of course, Christians oppose slavery, but this was the real world in which Peter taught. And so that God's truth could be communicated in God's way, the Spirit taught God's principles using the language and principles of that real world.

Even for servants, therefore, Peter says there was to be a submissive spirit. In this nation, we do not have *literal* slavery, but we do have *masters*—we call them bosses, and they can be bad.

Insight from Yesterday. In the Old Testament, Daniel was a man whose ordinary work brought great glory to God. He served God as a government employee under the supervision of an unsaved person. But in the final analysis, he served only *one* Master. He did not serve men during his prime time and God on his off-hours. He served God twenty-four hours a day, seven days a week.

Look in the Book of Daniel this week and get to know this godly man whose life stood apart for God. Daniel was in the world, but not of the world. He lived a pure life—not *isolating* himself from service, but *separating* himself unto holiness. He was salt and light. You don't put a lighthouse in the middle of downtown, and you don't put fish in one barrel and the salt in another.

Application for Today. You may feel that you are living and working in Babylon right now. God's name is taken in vain if taken at all. Obscene stories and raw cartoons are the order of the day. Those around you may flirt and dress provocatively. There may be incessant gossip, materialism, greed, and sinful ambitions. And on top of all this, your boss may be a slave driver.

What a terrific venue for demonstrating the power of God's ability to change! Any pagan can gripe. But what will you do with a "bad" boss?

Let 1 Peter 2:19 be your guide: "For this is *thankworthy,* if a man for conscience toward God endure grief, suffering wrongfully." Give thanks. It gives God glory.

If Christians would live like this on Monday, more people would believe what pastors preach on Sunday. When an employer goes to an agency to find potential employees, he should be saying, "I want a Christian worker. Do you have any? They're incredible! They arrive on time, they don't gossip, they don't steal, they're not lazy, and they treat me as if I were some kind of a god."

If you are in a difficult situation, let me give you some suggestions for being a lighthouse where you work:

1. *Do not brag.* "Let your light so shine before men, that they may see your good works, and glorify your Father which is in heaven" (Matt. 5:16). Notice that your light is to *glow,* not to *glare.* They are to see the light and not the lamp. Self-righteous people are obnoxious—especially at work.

2. *Do not nag.* If you nag, they will hate to see you coming. I know they are sinners. That's why they sin. That's what sinners do. But a sinner is never won by being talked down to. Colossians 4:5–6 says, "Walk in wisdom toward them that are without, redeeming the time. Let your speech be always with grace, seasoned with salt, that ye may know how ye ought to answer every man." Remember that the pulpit is the place for preaching.

3. *Do not lag.* Carry your part of the load and do a little more. It is a sin for a Christian to do less than his best. Ephesians 6:5–6 exhorts, "Servants, be obedient to them that are your masters according to the flesh, with fear and trembling, in singleness of your heart, as unto Christ; not with eyeservice, as menpleasers; but as the servants of Christ, doing the will of God from the heart." "And whatsoever ye do, do it heartily, as to the Lord, and not unto men; knowing that of the Lord ye shall receive the reward of the inheritance: for ye serve the Lord Christ" (Col. 3:23–24). And finally, "Let as many servants as are

under the yoke count their own masters worthy of all honour, that the name of God and his doctrine be not blasphemed" (1 Tim. 6:1).

4. *Do not sag.* Never let down in your Christian life. Refuse to compromise. Daniel was not self-righteous, but he refused to participate and dissipate with those who practiced a licentious lifestyle. Keep full of joy. Let the joy of the Lord be your strength. Store up his grace every morning before you go to work. Most people are not all that interested in going to heaven or hell. They want to know how to "hack it" on Monday. When they see your victory, they may come to you and want to know who put that song in your heart. Peter says then you will have an opportunity to share in a vibrant way (1 Pet. 3:15).

Wherever you work—be it an office, classroom, hospital, studio, factory, or in your home—you need to make your workplace a lighthouse for Jesus. Regardless of the conditions. Put some spiritual dynamite under the bridge that separates your work life from your worship life and ignite a holy fire of Shekinah glory that will illuminate every corner of your workplace!

3. Submission to Mean Mates. A third place where we encounter unworthy authorities is within the home. First Peter 3:1–2 tells wives to "be in subjection to your own husbands; that, if any obey not the word, they also may without the word be won by the conversation of the wives; while they behold your chaste conversation coupled with fear."

Peter goes on to say that wives should not let fashion or hairstyles be their chief adornment: "Whose adorning let it not be that outward adorning of plaiting the hair, and of wearing of gold, or of putting on of apparel; but let it be the hidden man of the heart, in that which is not corruptible, even the ornament of a meek and quiet spirit, which is in the sight of God of great price" (1 Pet. 3:3–4).

Let me clarify what Peter is saying. He is not against a woman making herself attractive. Remember ladies, your appearance is a part of your testimony. You will not *better influence* your unsaved husband by going around looking like an unmade bed. But the greatest witness is a submissive and serene spirit.

Just as Christians are to submit to secular authorities in government and the workplace, believing wives are to submit to pagan husbands. A home must have a head—there cannot be two heads.

We will talk about the home at length in a later chapter, but for now let me address what 1 Corinthians 11:3 teaches: "But I would have you know, that the head of every man is Christ; and the head of the woman is the man; and the head of Christ is God." The man is the head of the woman, Christ is the head of the man, and God the Father is the head of Christ.

This does not mean that the man is superior to the woman. The woman is no more inferior to her husband than Christ is to the Father. Submission occurs among equals. Galatians 3:28 tells us, "There is neither Jew nor Greek, there is neither bond nor free, there is neither male nor female: for ye are all one in Christ Jesus." In Christ, Jews and Greeks are equal, as well as slaves and masters and yes, male and female—all are one in Jesus, but authority still remains. Even in the case of a bad husband, as Ruth Graham says, "It's your job to love your husband; it is God's job to make him good."

THE PROBLEMS OF SUBMISSION

At this point, you've read about the principles and places of submission, but what about the problems of submission? What if your supervisor asks you to be involved in an unethical business practice? What if the government forbids us from studying our Bibles or from publicly saying a prayer? What if churches are commanded to ordain homosexuals? What if the teacher or the school board insists on using a vulgar or profane curriculum in your child's school?

It is then that we must understand that *submission is not always the same as obedience*. Ultimate authority belongs to God. We render to Caesar the things that are his and unto God the things that belong to God. Caesar must never be given what is God's. Francis Schaeffer wrote *A Christian Manifesto* in 1981. In it, he wrote at length about civil disobedience and disobedience. I appreciate this quote:

Has God set up an authority in the state that is autonomous from Himself? Are we to obey the state no matter what? Are we? In this one area is indeed Man the measure of all things? And I would answer, not at all, not at all.

When Jesus says in Matthew 22:21, "Give to Caesar what is Caesar's, and to God what is God's," it is not:

GOD and CAESAR

It was, is, and it always will be:

GOD
and
CAESAR[2]

For example, in Acts 5:28 the magistrates commanded the disciples to stop upsetting the status quo by their preaching. The apostles boldly responded: "We ought to obey God rather than men. The God of our fathers raised up Jesus, whom ye slew and hanged on a tree. Him hath God exalted with his right hand to be a Prince and a Saviour, for to give repentance to Israel, and forgiveness of sins. And we are his witnesses of these things; and so is also the Holy Ghost, whom God hath given to them that obey him" (Acts 5:29b–32).

They submitted to being thrown into jail, but they never stopped preaching.

What does it mean to "obey God rather than men"? Some of God's commands are qualifiable and some are unqualifiable. Romans 12:18 tells us, "If it be possible, as much as lieth in you, live peaceably with all men." But sometimes that's not possible because we can't control the actions of other men. We must be obedient, "as much as lieth in us." But when the time comes when we are commanded to do something against God's law and truth, we obey God rather than men.

John the Baptist submitted to his own beheading, but he never defied the headship of Christ. He lost one head by honoring another

Head. Daniel prayed though it was against the law. The Egyptian midwives would not kill the male babies though Pharaoh commanded it.

There may come a time for civil disobedience. Christians working in hospitals should refuse to be a part of the grisly abortion business. The principle of submission to God always takes priority over any lesser commandment or principle. We should never use the lesser as an occasion to break the greater, and we should never use the greater as a needless excuse to break the lesser.

The state is within its rights to demand that our church buildings meet fire codes and that our buses pass inspection. Our disobedience against the state should only involve matters that are strictly dealing with religious liberty. To resist the state in matters not dealing with religious liberty puts us in the position of resisting God and fighting against him.

Also, we need to learn that civil disobedience is not anarchy or mob rule. There is no warrant for Christians to create mobs and chaos in order to achieve a seemingly spiritual purpose.

For example, the cause of Jesus has suffered because of the violation of the properties of abortion clinics. Tragically, some who justify violence against property (bombing) do not discriminate in their anger. They also find it easy to justify violence against the *persons* in these clinics who are abortionists. Some have even carried out murder in the name of God.

The power to punish murderers is a civil power, not an ecclesiastical or personal power. Did you know that the early church was against abortion and severely disciplined those who were guilty of it? They took a strong stand—rescuing babies and counseling women in trouble. Never once did they suggest violence as a recourse to the abortion problem.

Yet while Christians are not anarchists, they are not to be compromisers either. The Bible does not teach unqualified obedience to evil government or unlimited submission to evil persons.

Before you choose the route of civil disobedience, you might consider the following questions:

- Do you have a clear Bible mandate based on balanced interpretation?
- Have you earnestly prayed and sought spiritual guidance?
- Have you sought godly counsel from wise leaders?
- Have you exhausted every avenue of appeal?
- Is your spirit one of a rebel or one who acts from a broken heart?
- Have you counted the cost of your actions?

Let me say a word about our involvement in politics. We must never identify the church with any political party. We need to pray for all parties and encourage them to repent and turn to God. The church is neither the state's servant nor its master; it is the state's conscience.

We will be civil but never silent. The Bible is filled with examples of God's spokesmen tweaking the conscience of rulers: Nathan, Elijah, Daniel, Eliazar, and even Moses before Pharaoh.

The church and the Christian not only *can* but *must speak out* on the abortion holocaust. The blood of these martyred little ones is on our nation's hands. We must cry out when we hear attempts to normalize sodomy, distribute condoms in our schools, and prohibit Christians from praying aloud in public places. It has well been said that nothing is politically right that is morally wrong. Government is for the purpose of restraining evil, not restraining good. The ideal is a free church in a free state.

But what about freedom in marriage? What if a wife is being physically abused by her husband? In my opinion she has the freedom to leave that situation immediately. I believe she should get away to a place of safety until it is clear that he has changed. While she should have a submissive spirit, she should never submit to battering. In the case of spousal abuse, God's higher law takes precedence over the authority of the unworthy husband.

HOW TO BEHAVE IN A CAVE

A classic example of staying submissive to authority while yet seeking shelter is David in the Old Testament. As the king of Israel, Saul had authority over David. Yet Saul was insane with jealousy and determined that David should be put to death. All of the energies of the kingdom were brought to one burning focus—Kill David! Kill David!

To save his life, David fled from Saul, who was his authority. But he still kept a submissive spirit.

While hiding in a cave at Engeddi, David noticed Saul coming in to relieve himself. In the darkness Saul did not see David. Those with David thought it was too good an opportunity to miss. Just one stroke of the sword—and good-bye to poverty, persecution, reproaches, and sneers. And David could say hello to triumph, riches, power, and praise.

But David knew how to behave in a cave. Notice how he respected the authority of Saul. "And David said to Abishai, Destroy him not: for who can stretch forth his hand against the LORD's anointed, and be guiltless?" (1 Sam. 26:9)

David did not submit himself to being killed by Saul. Instead, he separated himself from danger *while* keeping a submissive spirit.

Remember the wife whom I told you about earlier in this chapter? She told God, "I truly want to do your will. If it is to stay, I will stay, relying on your grace and strength. If it is to leave, I will leave, relying on your courage and wisdom."

Now let me finish her letter:

Three weeks later the verbal abuse began and I felt in my spirit it was time to go. Whatever held me there in previous times was gone. I removed myself from the abusive situation. I did not turn my back on my marriage, but I left with the hopes of exerting pressure on my husband to go to counseling with me and to face the rage in his own heart so that he and I along with our children could have a godly family.

My husband had refused counseling in the past. . . . Now praise the Lord due to my firm action and God's grace my husband and I are in counseling, and he is now a very willing participant. He is learning about the Spirit-filled life, and I am greatly encouraged about the changes I see in him. We are still separated because after six years of abuse, I'm finding so much buried hurt and pain, I need more time to heal than I imagined. But our relationship in some ways is better than ever.

I beg you please in some way address what to do in actually *abusive* situations. I realize what a tight line you must walk, not wanting to give a woman an "out" to leave her husband when that would not be God's will. But I know that there are women out there like myself who so desperately want to do the right thing and please God and will be listening next week concerning what to do. Perhaps in my situation it was all in God's timing—his perfect timing—and my marriage will now be healed.

What a precious spirit I sensed in this dear woman. My prayer is for continued healing in her home. She committed her way to the Lord—submitting to him in obedience. And God blessed—blessing always follows obedience.

Here are some questions that a wife should ask before disobeying her husband's headship:

- Have I already been living in loving and wholehearted submission to my husband?
- Has he ever actually commanded me to do something wrong?
- Are the children or am I in danger of physical, emotional, or sexual abuse?
- Do I have a spirit of rebellion? Could it be that I am doing a right thing with a wrong spirit?

Remember, there is never an excuse for disrespect.

THE PRICE OF SUBMISSION

Submission has a price. According to 1 Peter 2:19–23, it is good to endure grief and wrongful suffering with patience for the sake of God:

> For this is thankworthy, if a man for conscience toward God endure grief, suffering wrongfully. For what glory is it, if, when ye be buffeted for your faults, ye shall take it patiently? but if, when ye do well, and suffer for it, ye take it patiently, this is acceptable with God. For even hereunto were ye called: because Christ also suffered for us, leaving us an example, that ye should follow his steps: who did no sin, neither was guile found in his mouth: who, when he was reviled, reviled not again; when he suffered, he threatened not; but committed himself to him that judgeth righteously.

Jesus is the ultimate example of grief and wrongful suffering—enduring with patience for the glory of God. Jesus is the doctor who took the patient's illness, then paid the hospital bill. Was it fair? No. And all the more did it bring God the glory.

Jesus left us an example to follow. He experienced undeserved suffering (1 Pet. 2:22), unretaliated suffering (2:23), and unfrustrated suffering (2:23). The word *committed* in the above passage shows that he handed himself over to the one who would make it right in his own way and in his own time.

We receive supernatural power and authority when we submit to earthly powers—especially evil ones. The Holy Spirit longs to give each of us the Kingdom Authority that the early church exercised. They overcame the world. They toppled the greatest military dynasty the world has ever known. They turned the world upside down by not overtly resisting evil but by refusing to give in to it. Their lack of sinful resistance shut the mouths of their accusers, took the swords from their hands, and chased them from their thrones.

How much quicker might our victory be? Whenever we submit to the authorities God has established, we receive the Kingdom Authority against which evil cannot stand. Then we become overcomers of evil—triumphant over all the powers of darkness through the power of God. We can have victory in our homes, in our businesses, in our schools, and in our personal lives. Jesus is calling you to that victory. What will you do?

I wish I could have learned something of the spirit of submission long ago. When I was in high school, I played football. It was about the only sport I was any good at. We had a great football team, and I had a great coach, but he was a profane man. I was a Christian boy. I had just given my heart to the Lord. This coach had a way of taking the cigarette out of his mouth and throwing it on the ground, stamping it with his foot, and taking off his hat with the other hand and throwing it on the ground, then kicking it. He would then let out a string of oaths when someone had done something wrong. It used to grieve me to hear my Lord and Savior's name taken in vain.

And while we practiced after school, this coach also had the idea that we ought to practice on Sundays from time to time. There was something in me that said, "I'm not going to practice on Sundays." I believed that I ought to be in the house of God on Sundays, so I refused to go to practice on the Lord's Day. One day, this coach told his psychology class that Rogers was using religion to get out of things that he didn't want to do. The truth of the matter was that I loved football almost too much. I wanted to be there, but there was something in me that said I ought not to be there, but that I ought to be in the house of God on Sunday.

When I heard, however, that he had said this to his psychology class, it flew all over me. I decided that no one else had ever talked back to the coach, but one fellow was going to. I met him in the locker room. I said, "Coach, I want you to hear something. I am tired of the way you talk on the football field. I am a Christian, and I resent you taking my Lord's name in vain. You are not going to talk to me that way any more. And I want to say another thing. I resent your saying that I use religion as an excuse to get out of doing things that I don't want to do. That is not true. I am Christian, and Jesus Christ means more to me than football. And now I want to say a third thing. I quit the team."

He said, "What?"

I said, "You heard me. I quit."

He said, "You can't quit."

I said, "I can quit, and I have quit."

He said, "If you quit, you'll be letting your teammates down, letting your coaches down, letting your school down, and you'll be letting this community down."

I said, "I'd rather let you all down than let Jesus down." Then I turned around and walked off.

For a number of years, I thought I had done the right thing. But since I've gotten older, I've had a change of mind. I wish I could go back and talk to that coach again and speak to him more respectfully. I wish I could have gone there with a broken heart and given my testimony and not been so cocky and arrogant. I thought I was so right, and yet I was so wrong because I had the spirit of a rebel.

An attitude of submission is truly a mark of a Spirit-filled life.

PART III

Exercising the Power of Kingdom Authority

CHAPTER 8

THE AUTHORITY OF JESUS' NAME

The key to all Kingdom Authority is the lordship of Jesus Christ. He is the King who can rightly say, "All power is given unto me in heaven and in earth" (Matt. 28:18). Therefore, Paul rightly said that Jesus is Lord both of the dead and the living.

> For none of us liveth to himself, and no man dieth to himself. For whether we live, we live unto the Lord; and whether we die, we die unto the Lord: whether we live therefore, or die, we are the Lord's. For to this end Christ both died, and rose, and revived, that he might be Lord both of the dead and living. But why dost thou judge thy brother? or why dost thou set at nought thy brother? for we shall all stand before the judgment seat of Christ. For it is written, As I live, saith the Lord, every knee shall bow to me, and every tongue shall confess to God. So then every one of us shall give account of himself to God (Rom. 14:7–12).

In the church of Rome to which Paul wrote, an outburst of criticism and judgment had begun. The bickering and judgment revolved around issues about which there is room for disagreement: days, diets, and deportment. Paul wrote them to say, "Get off one another's backs! Cut the criticism! It is not your opinion of someone that counts, or their opinion of you; you both belong to Jesus—and Jesus is Lord!"

Look up the definition of that word. A lord is one with absolute power, absolute authority. We often speak of commitment, but the real issue is surrender. Remember when you're committed, you're in control; when you surrender, you relinquish control. We can commit to win souls, study the Bible, and tithe. But if a thug puts a gun to your head, you don't commit your wallet; you surrender it. Christians need to go beyond commitment to surrender because Jesus is Lord and he ruled not with a weapon but a scepter of love.

After a great naval battle, the French admiral came aboard Admiral Nelson's British ship to surrender with his hand outstretched. But Nelson said, "Your sword first, sir." Before we embrace the Lord Jesus, we have to lay down our swords. We have to put away our agendas. We have to pry our fingers from the things we clench. Jesus is Lord of all of them now.

To understand that truth is the beginning of Kingdom Authority. He is called *Lord* no less than 747 times in the New Testament. You can't make him *Lord;* He already owns that title. Romans 14:9 says that he died and rose that he might be Lord of the living and the dead. Acts 2:36 says, "God hath made that same Jesus, whom ye have crucified, both Lord and Christ." You don't do that; God did it. Your questions are, first, will you recognize his lordship, and second, will you submit to it? He is Lord of all you have and all you do; He is Lord of your words and thoughts, of your time and testimony. Do you live by that lordship?

THE REDEEMING CLAIM OF HIS LORDSHIP

Jesus' claim for lordship is simple: He died for us. He gave his life to claim us as Lord. In the manner of his death he was purchasing us. As the price for ownership of you and me, he spent the currency of his own blood, the jewels of his tears. That truth undercuts any illusion of independence we may foster. "What? know ye not that your body is the temple of the Holy Ghost which is in you, which ye have of God, and ye are not your own?" (1 Cor. 6:19). You do not belong to yourself if you're a Christian. You are a purchased possession.

There is no shortage of people claiming to be Christians. Throngs have walked down church aisles or been through the baptistry. But is Jesus Lord in a real way to those people? When we acknowledge and live under the rule of Jesus as Lord, we are under new management. The decision to give your heart to Jesus is the last independent legitimate decision you ever make. Is that statement unsettling? It should be wonderful and exciting! After all, who can better manage our lives: the Lord of Creation, or we ourselves? He knows what is best for us, and what we ourselves would do if we were wise enough to see things from his perspective.

God has made a big investment in us. When one makes a big investment, he is careful to protect that investment. God's investment in you is a blessing, because you can be sure *he will protect his investment.* Ephesians 1:13–14 speaks of God's children. "In whom ye also trusted, after that ye heard the word of truth, the gospel of your salvation: in whom also after that ye believed, ye were sealed with that holy Spirit of promise, which is the earnest of our inheritance until the redemption of the *purchased possession,* unto the praise of his glory."

You are the purchased possession! God bought you with a price, and he put a mark or seal on you—a mark called the Holy Spirit. In New Testament times, a seal marked a legal document. A king would create a document, put melted wax on it, and use his signet ring to make a seal. This marked it as the property of the king. Paul has precisely that custom in mind here when he refers to you as God's property, sealed with the Spirit to mark the transaction so no mistake will be made. It is legal and binding. Satan is defeated, and the Spirit seals the promise.

One who does not have Jesus as Lord of his life cannot call himself a Christian. Salvation is yielding to the lordship of Christ: "That if thou shalt confess with thy mouth the Lord Jesus, and shalt believe in thine heart that God hath raised him from the dead, thou shalt be saved. For with the heart man believeth unto righteousness; and with the mouth confession is made unto salvation" (Rom. 10:9–10). This means more than saying the right words.

When Paul wrote this passage, those words could cost a man his life. Caesar was more than emperor; he was proclaimed god. Citizens were required by law to proclaim the same. Other gods could be spoken for, but Caesar had to be included in the deal. Christians would not do that, even at the point of the sword. It would have been easy to give in, but the early believers knew there was no middle ground. *Christ is Lord of all or not Lord at all.*

We do not take Christ "as Savior"; we can only take him as "Lord and Savior." In the same way, when people marry, the "I do" signifies their acceptance of a lawfully wedded husband and wife. When I married, I did not take Joyce "as housekeeper" or "as anything" I took Joyce—all of her. And we take Jesus—all of him—Master (Lord), mediator (Jesus), and Messiah (Christ).

We may not fully understand all that the concept of marriage entails, and we may spend the rest of this life discovering it; but we are binding ourselves, committing and surrendering ourselves to that bond. We don't say, "I do" with fingers crossed behind our backs; we don't accept Jesus with any reservations. He surrendered on Calvary without reservation. We will not have what he gives until we accept who he is: He is Lord!

Charles Haddon Spurgeon, the great preacher, put it this way:

> If the convert declares that he knows the Lord's will but doesn't mean to attend to it, it is your duty to assure him that he is not saved. Don't imagine that the Gospel is magnified, or God glorified, by going to worldlings and telling them that they may be saved at this moment simply by accepting Christ as their Savior, while they are wedded to their idols with their hearts, and their hearts are still in love with sin. If I do so, I tell them a lie, I pervert the Gospel, I insult Christ, I turn the grace of God into lasciviousness.

It is not Christ *and;* it is Christ *or.* He died for us, and that is the redeeming claim of his lordship.

THE RESURRECTION CONQUEST OF HIS LORDSHIP

In Romans 14:9 we read, "To this end Christ both died, and rose." In those two actions we see the redeeming claim and the resurrection conquest. When he died, he gave himself for us, but when he rose, he gave himself to us to live within us. This means three things.

TOTAL SUBMISSION

First, it means our total submission. No man can serve two masters. Jesus is no part-time king. He must be Lord of all to be Lord at all, so you are committed to Jesus Christ completely and exclusively.

ABSOLUTE OWNERSHIP

Second, it means his absolute ownership of all that you possess. When someone owned a slave, he also owned that slave's possessions. Jesus is not simply the owner of a church member's tithe. He doesn't own 10 percent of a Christian's wealth; he owns it all. The tithe is simply a tangible expression of that. It is a symbol of all our resources, all our time, all our intellect, all our relationships, and all our deepest desires.

UNQUESTIONED OBEDIENCE

Third, it means unquestioned obedience. In Luke 6:46 Jesus asked, "Why call ye me, Lord, Lord, and do not the things which I say?" Being a Christian means obedience in every area—our work, our witness, our friendships, our families, our recreation. The flesh may fear that kind of obedience. Yet, how foolish to fear the one who died for us!

Imagine you have a teenage son. He comes into the room and says, "Mom and Dad, I've been thinking and praying about things, and I've decided I want to be a totally obedient son. It seems logical that since you're more experienced, you're wiser about life. I know you would give your lives for me, and you only want the best for me. So I'm going to trust you and do whatever you think is best." Would you go into the next room with your spouse, chuckle gleefully, and start planning to make your son's life miserable? Never! Chances are that if you were thinking of buying him a new bike, that may tip the scales in his favor.

God is the perfect parent; he wants your fulfillment, which comes only in complete faith and trust in his will. Don't be afraid to obey him without question.

THE REGAL CONFESSION OF HIS LORDSHIP

There must also be the regal confession of his lordship. In Romans 14:11 Paul goes on to say that the time will come when all people will bow down and confess his name. "Every knee shall bow to me, and every tongue shall confess to God."

It's going to happen sooner or later: you will confess Christ as Lord now or in the next world. Philippians 2:10–11 describes that same eventuality. "That at the name of Jesus every knee should bow, of things in heaven, and things in earth, and things under the earth; and that every tongue should confess that Jesus Christ is Lord, to the glory of God the Father." Things in heaven: the angels. Things in earth: the humans. Things under the earth: the devil and his demons. The saints of all ages will bow. Every king and ruler will say, "Jesus is Lord." Hitler and Saddam Hussein will say it. Satan himself will bow on his thorny, twisted knees and confess that Jesus Christ is Lord!

But you don't need to wait until that great day of history's culmination. If I could say only three more words before losing the ability to speak forever, these three words would be "JESUS IS LORD." Indeed, this is the most glorious of all truths.

The name of the Lord Jesus is therefore the first principle in getting an upper hand on the underworld. The early Christians were few in number, meager in finances, and they had no social position or political power. But one thing they did have—THE NAME.

The Book of Acts tells how these new Christians used the name of Jesus to shatter Satan's strongholds with the force that a white-hot cannonball would use to shatter a crate of eggs. In this one book there are thirty-two references to that blessed name. Look at a few:

- Salvation Is in His Name—Acts 2:21
- Healing Is in His Name—Acts 3:6
- Demons Flee at His Name—Acts 16:18
- Baptism Is in His Name—Acts 19:5
- Saints Will Die for His Name—Acts 12:1–13

How then do we exercise Kingdom Authority? In the name of the Lord Jesus Christ. Before I say more on this, let me remind you that in the Bible the name stands for the person and *that person's authority.* This is also true today. When a man puts his name on a check, this gives the bank the right to give the holder of that check some of that man's money. The name stands for the person who has put his name on the check. If the check bounces, they don't put the check in jail. They put the man who put his name on the check in jail.

WE PRAY IN THE NAME OF JESUS

"If ye shall ask any thing in my name, I will do it" (John 14:14). When we have his name legitimately behind our prayers, we're praying with Kingdom Authority. A prayer with Jesus' name behind it is like a bonafide purchase order that would be honored by heaven.

The sad thing, however, is that the name of Jesus is often forged to a prayer by one who has not sought or surrendered to Jesus Christ's lordship. The name of Jesus is not a magical formula that somehow sanitizes and energizes a prayer. True prayer must be mandated by heaven. I'm convinced that the only prayer that gets to heaven is the prayer that starts in heaven. We close the circuit when we pray in faith in the name of Jesus.

The key to praying in the name of Jesus is to hear from heaven. Jesus himself exercised authority by hearing from heaven. Jesus laid aside his divine prerogatives and acted as obedient man. "Then answered Jesus and said unto them, Verily, verily, I say unto you, The Son can do nothing of himself, but what he seeth the Father do: for what things soever he doeth, these also doeth the Son likewise" (John 5:19).

Jesus did not "pull rank" on us. Had he done that, he could not have been our example.

But he is our example. "As my Father hath sent me, even so send I you" (John 20:21b). Therefore, my great need is not more authority, but more intimacy with Jesus so I can coordinate my will with his. Is what I am asking in line with his will? Is this what he wants?

I am convinced that we would move into incredible realms of power and Kingdom Authority if we would do as Jesus did with the Father. We would spend time listening to him, to get his instructions, and to line up our wills with his.

Another equal tragedy is not the misuse of the name of Jesus, but the omission of his name. There seems to be a desire in today's society to remove the name of Jesus from public prayers. It does not seem to be polite or politically correct to pray openly and publicly in his name.

God forbid that we should be ashamed of the name of Jesus in the public arena. I've noticed that those who lecture much about pluralism in religion really don't mean it. If they did, they would want a Christian to pray as a Christian prays, a Jew to pray as he normally prays, and a Buddhist to pray as he normally prays. What they call "pluralism" is really synchronism—a dumbing down and melding together of all religions. Author and columnist Nicholas von Hoffmann wrote these words:

> The Mush God has been known to appear to millionaires on golf courses. He appears to politicians at ribbon-cutting ceremonies and to clergymen speaking the invocation on national television at either a Democratic or Republican convention.
>
> The Mush God has no theology to speak of, being a cream of wheat divinity. The Mush God has no particular credo, no tenets of faith, nothing that would make it difficult for a believer and nonbeliever alike to lower one's head when the temporary chairman tells us that "Reverend, Rabbi, Father, Mufti, or So-And-So will lead us in an innocuous, harmless prayer." For this god at public occasions is not a jealous god.

You can even invoke him to start a hookers' convention and he/she won't be offended.

God of the Rotary, the Optimist Club, Protector of the Buddy System, the Mush God is the Lord of the secular, ritual, of the necessary, but hypocritical forms and formalities that hush the divisive and the derisive. The Mush God is a serviceable god whose laws are chiseled, not on tablets, but written on sand, open to amendment, qualification, and erasure. This is a god who will compromise with you, make allowances and declare all wars holy, all peaces hallowed.

We Serve in the Name of Jesus

And whatsoever ye do in word or deed, do all in the name of the Lord Jesus, giving thanks to God and the Father by him. Wives, submit yourselves unto your own husbands, as it is fit in the Lord. Husbands, love your wives, and be not bitter against them. Children, obey your parents in all things: for this is well pleasing unto the Lord. Fathers, provoke not your children to anger, lest they be discouraged. Servants, obey in all things your masters according to the flesh; not with eyeservice, as menpleasers; but in singleness of heart, fearing God: and whatsoever ye do, do it heartily, as to the Lord, and not unto men; knowing that of the Lord ye shall receive the reward of the inheritance: for ye serve the Lord Christ (Col. 3:17–24).

We're to live every day in the power and authority of the name of Jesus. In the verses that follow, this command to do all in the name of Jesus exhibits some everyday examples.

- Wives submit to their husbands in the name of Jesus—verse 18
- Husbands love in the name of Jesus—verse 19
- Children obey in the name of Jesus—verse 20
- Parents raise children in the name of Jesus—verse 21
- Workers serve in the name of Jesus—verse 22–24

Such everyday use of the name of Jesus does not trivialize that name. To the contrary, Scripture teaches: "Whether therefore ye eat, or drink, or whatsoever ye do, do all to the glory of God" (1 Cor. 10:31).

WE WAR IN THE NAME OF JESUS

"And the seventy returned again with joy, saying, Lord, even the devils are subject unto us *through thy name*. And he said unto them, I beheld Satan as lightning fall from heaven. Behold, I give unto you power to tread on serpents and scorpions, and over all the power of the enemy: and nothing shall by any means hurt you" (Luke 10:17–19).

Indeed, there is a name that sends shudders through the murky realms of the underworld. We may not have greater power than Satan, but we do have greater authority through the name. I have seen the power of the name in open warfare with Satan.

The setting was Hyderabad, India. I had spoken to a crowd of some fifty thousand in a soccer stadium. Then an Indian evangelist preached with power and was calling men and women to Christ. There was a great moving of the Spirit, and literally thousands were openly confessing Christ.

I was on the platform observing and rejoicing when I became aware of a disturbance. There was a man to my left who was writhing on the ground like a snake and then convulsing in unbelievable contortions. A small crowd stood in a circle around this man, not daring to get close.

As I watched, it was evident that this was an open attack of Satan upon him. This man was being violently tormented by a demon spirit. I had no desire to get involved and honestly felt somewhat fearful. I breathed a prayer and left the platform and went to the disturbance. I knelt beside this man, put my hands on him, and prayed, "In the name of Jesus, I rebuke this spirit. Come out of this man and leave him." At that moment, he went limp and fell to the ground. I took him by the hand and lifted him up. He put his head upon my shoulder and wept softly almost like a little child. I gave him a compassionate hug and prayed for him.

He didn't understand my English nor did I his Telugu, but one thing I know: the powers of darkness understood the greater authority of the magnificent name of Jesus. At this point, let me warn against presumption and secondhand religion in the battle with demons. In the Book of Acts, we see a sad example of this.

> Then certain of the vagabond Jews, exorcists, took upon them to call over them which had evil spirits the name of the Lord Jesus, saying, We adjure you by Jesus whom Paul preacheth. And there were seven sons of one Sceva, a Jew, and chief of the priests, which did so. And the evil spirit answered and said, Jesus I know, and Paul I know; but who are ye? And the man in whom the evil spirit was leaped on them, and overcame them, and prevailed against them, so that they fled out of that house naked and wounded. And this was known to all the Jews and Greeks also dwelling at Ephesus; and fear fell on them all, and the name of the Lord Jesus was magnified (Acts 19:13–17).

These seven men "took upon them" this ministry. It was evident that they were imitating the apostle Paul and appealing to the "Jesus whom Paul preacheth." It was not the Jesus they knew, but Paul's Jesus. It was secondhand religion. The result was disaster. Satan sneers at religion without reality. I recall an interesting little allegorical poem on the topic:

> A tiger met a lion as they set beside a pool.
> Said the tiger to the lion, "Why are you roaring like a fool?"
> "That's not foolish," said the lion, with a twinkle in his eyes,
> They call me the king of all beasts because I advertise.
>
> A rabbit heard them talking, ran on like a streak.
> He thought he would try the lion's plan, but his roar was just a squeak.
> A fox came to investigate and had lunch in the woods,

And so my friend, when you advertise, be sure you've got the goods.

This is especially true in spiritual warfare. When we are under the lordship of Jesus, we have the goods. God releases all the authority of heaven to believers.

Thank God for the power of the blessed name of Jesus. A colaborer gave me a beautifully framed poem that exalts his name. It hangs in my study near the door. I often read it just before I go out to preach.

> There is a name, a wondrous name,
> Of infinite and endless fame,
> Of God beloved, by saints revered,
> By angels and archangels feared,
> Ordained by God, 'ere the world began,
> Revealed by angels unto man,
> Proclaimed by men, believed, adored,
> By hearts and prayer and praise outpoured.
> The theme of prophets, priests, and kings,
> The Word of which sweet psalmists sing,
> By pilgrims blessed, by suff'ers sung,
> The last word breathed by martyr's tongue,
> The name most precious and sublime,
> Supreme in faith, supreme in time,
> Destined to live and conquer all,
> 'Til all knees everywhere shall fall
> And tongue confess—what God proclaimed—
> This name to be the name of names,
> The name which in high heaven will be
> The one name of eternity:
> Then, oh my soul, its praise forth tell
> Jesus—the name ineffable!

CHAPTER 9

THE AUTHORITY OF THE WORD OF GOD

Early in my Christian life, I ran into the issue of biblical authority headlong.

I got my first taste of theological liberalism when I attended a denominational college on a football and ministerial scholarship. As I contemplated my options for my course of study, I was encouraged by the faculty advisor *not* to major in religion because I would get all of that in postgraduate studies in a seminary. Instead, he suggested that I should study history, journalism, or another of the liberal arts.

Yet my eager mind refused to wait. I wanted "megadoses" of Bible truth right then! I stayed true to my conviction and majored in religion. With eager anticipation I attended my first lecture.

The religion professor began something like this: "Young people, there are three major schools of theology." I picked up my pen ready to write. "First, there are the 'fun-damn-mentalists.' Too much fun, too much damn, and not enough mental." Well, I thought, I don't want to be one of those.

Then the winsome professor continued, "Next, there are the mod-durn-ists." He was speaking of modernism, which is just a cosmopolitan twist on the less cerebral "liberalism." He went on to explain all the excesses and errors of modernism that has jettisoned the vital truths of the faith. He implied that they were "durn" wrong. For this young preacher, that settled the issue. I didn't want to be a "fundamentalist" or a "modernist."

Finally the professor smiled and said there was third school of thought called "neoorthodoxy" that was a wise compromise between the other two extremes. In neoorthodoxy, he explained, we didn't have to believe all of the miracles and historical accounts in the Bible, but we could still hold the great truths that the modernists had thrown overboard. The answer was neoorthodoxy!

I later learned what neoorthodoxy is. It began as a reaction to modern liberalism. It responded to the liberal emphasis that Jesus was only an enlightened man by emphasizing the sovereignty of God and his difference with man. It was sort of a "halfway" house between abject liberalism and Bible belief. It teaches that the *Bible is not the objective Word of God* because God cannot be known by mere human words. Rather, the Bible is a channel through which man may encounter God. The Bible is unique, but it is human and can err; and it only imperfectly gives us a glimpse of truth.

This is so confusing because many times the neoorthodox scholar will use commonly accepted biblical terms but put his own meaning on those terms. "They use our words and their dictionary."

I was speaking to a professor from that college about the resurrection. We were having wonderful fellowship during the Easter season until I discovered that he did not believe in the empty tomb. Both of us were talking about resurrection, but he meant something totally different. He did not believe that Jesus walked out of the tomb.

It is so hard to get hold of. According to neoorthodoxy, the Bible is not the Word of God in a clear-cut meaning. Yet it is the Word of God in the sense that it *becomes* the Word of God by spiritual impact. But even then, it is full of mistakes and myths. This is theological "smoke and mirrors." What isn't, is; and what is, isn't.

They say, "To believe in a bodily resurrection may be beside the point for the Christian faith. The important thing is that in Jesus we can believe in the resurrection." It is a way of having the doctrine without having to be bothered about the facts on which the doctrine is built. It is a house without a foundation, floating on air!

This was heady stuff. At first, I said to myself, "That's what I am. I am neoorthodox." It was attractive and appealing to my impressionable mind for a semester or two. Then questions began to hound my mental doorstep. The Holy Spirit began a disquieting work in my heart and mind as I began to grapple with what I believe about the Word of God.

I came to a fork in the road—either the professor was right and the Bible was wrong, or the Bible was right and the professor was wrong. I determined to find out which was which by beginning a parallel study to my regular course work.

By now I had married my high school sweetheart, Joyce. When I told her of my plans, she responded, "You're not going to graduate if you try to take two courses at a time." Nonetheless, I persisted and bought some other books and began to study. Praise be to God, he guided my steps to his truth, and I learned that I was not neoorthodox after all, but instead a "dreaded" fundamentalist.

I hesitate to use the word *fundamentalist* because it conjures up ugly images in most people's minds. Plus, the word has lost much of its original meaning. Today, most people caricature a fundamentalist Christian as someone who is rigid, hate-filled, arrogant, and fanatical. Of course, if that's what it means to be a fundamentalist, then count me out.

From this point forward, I'd like us to consider the original essence of the word *fundamentalist*. The *Merriam-Webster Collegiate Dictionary* (1998) defines *fundamentalism* as a Protestant religious movement "emphasizing the literally interpreted Bible as fundamental to Christian life and teaching" and "a movement or attitude stressing strict adherence to a set of basic principles." A Christian fundamentalist is someone who believes the basic fundamentals of the faith—the inspiration of the Scriptures, the virgin birth of Jesus, his full deity, his blood atonement, his bodily resurrection, and his actual visible bodily return to this earth.

Have you ever wondered why Christians who believe in basics are criticized for being fundamentalists? What about football players who believe in the basic offensive and defensive principles of football—blocking, tackling, kicking, and so forth? Have you ever heard a sports-caster criticize an athlete for being a fundamentalist? It's all right for football—just not for Christianity, it would seem.

If emphasizing the inerrancy of the Word of God and seeking to adhere to his principles makes me a fundamentalist, then so be it. I choose to cling to the fundamentals of the faith and to the Word of the King regardless of public opinion. I am not ashamed to lift high the banner of Jesus and his truth. I believed these fundamental truths with all of my heart as a college student, and I still believe them today. However, the word *fundamentalist* has been so tarnished and distorted and loaded with baggage that I now just refer to myself as a Bible-believing Christian.

THE ISSUE IS AUTHORITY

We cannot live victoriously in spiritual warfare without an authoritative word from our supreme commander. "If the trumpet gives an uncertain sound, who will prepare himself to the battle?" Is the sound I hear a sound for a charge or retreat? Is it "Reveille," "Taps," or is it merely the wind in the trees? Perhaps it's a trumpet being blown by the adversary. Who knows?

Kingdom Authority and the authority of the Word of God are inextricably interwoven. It stands to reason that we cannot live in powerful and conquering confidence without a sure word from God.

From New Testament times, Christians have been confronted by the question of authority. "By what authority doest thou these things?" were the words with which they challenged the Lord Jesus Christ (see Matt. 21:23–24).

Indeed, there must be a final source of authority. Someone has to speak the last word to settle points of difference and establish what must be done. Without a settled word from the King there is continual confusion.

There are only three possible sources of authority in spiritual and religious matters. One, the individual conscience. Two, the church that expresses itself either through an assembly, a conference, a pope, or some other way. And three, Jesus Christ, who speaks through the inspired and infallible Scripture. I believe in the last of these.

Yet to say Scripture is a guide is not quite enough. Satan has endeavored to muddy the waters in the issue of biblical authority. There are four basic views about Scripture held in churches today.

LIBERAL VIEW

This view says that the Bible is *man's word* about God and other religious matters. It contains experiences and stories of pious men and can be described as a collection of religious experiences and insights. Liberalism got its start in the Garden of Eden with Satan's insidious "hath God said?" Basically defined, it does not accept the Bible as the Word of God.

When we speak of a "liberal" in theology, we are not describing someone who is merely a free thinker or open-minded. It is a movement that seeks to de-supernaturalize the Christian faith, especially with reference to miracles. Its focus is not on heaven, but on earth. Redemption is not the soul being saved by the shed blood of Jesus Christ, but rather the reconciliation of social groups and other like matters. In my estimation, it is an attempt to make the world a better place to go to hell from.

Liberalism has now descended into an even lower level called Postmodernism. A liberal or modernist confidence in a naturalistic reason has now dissipated. While we might think this is good, what follows may be even worse. Postmodernism is a worldview that tries to do without fixed truth altogether. Postmodernists construct their beliefs so what is true for one person may not be true for another. Truth, as they say, is relative or nonexistent. Morality depends on the individual's choice.

I was recently handed an article from a Nashville newspaper about a lecture at Vanderbilt University. The speaker, Marcus Borg, who was to speak at the divinity school's Benton Chapel, is also the author of *Meeting Jesus for the First Time.* Here are some choice quotes from that newspaper article:

> Pressures of religious diversity and scientific outlook are too strong for literalism to stay plausible, says scholar Marcus Borg. That's not bad news for the faith, he insists. Millions are building a Christian faith by embracing Jesus' virgin birth and his walking-on-water miracles as metaphors, not historical facts.
>
> In the current "battle" for Jesus being waged in seminaries and churches over the nature of Scripture and meaning of Jesus, Borg sides with the "millions who can't be literalists anymore. Maybe they tried to be literalists, but they can't believe Jesus is the only way to salvation," he said in an interview this week.
>
> "A major de-literalization is going on in the mainline churches, and it's irreversible." That doesn't mean they are losing their faith, he argued. He counts himself as one whose faith is strengthened by embracing the symbolic power of New Testament stories and the resurrection. That means a life transformed by a present relationship with God, not by disputed "facts" that happened in the New Testament era long ago. "For me, metaphor is more important than the literal," he said.
>
> "A weakness of the modern period, a blind spot among conservatives and liberals, is we're too preoccupied with factuality, saying it's true only if it's factual," Borg said. "We have a tin ear for metaphor; we dismiss it, like it's pretty language for something that could be said more directly. One task of theology in our time is to recover the power of the metaphor. Making doctrinal statements about Jesus—his virgin birth, his

physical resurrection—is not as important as seeing Christian faith as a path of personal transformation, a relationship with God today," he said.

He said Easter, the story of Jesus' resurrection, shouldn't be a debate about whether the tomb was empty or not. "At Easter, Jesus continued to be experienced by his followers after his death. That experience took a variety of forms— visions, a sense of his presence, or they still experienced the power of healing in Jesus. Those kinds of experiences go on to this day. Something about Easter led them to say, 'Jesus is Lord.'"

May the Lord have mercy!

The rejection of truth in Postmodernism means that attempts to persuade are construed as acts of oppressive power. Since in this view everyone's beliefs have equal validity, then I don't have the right to impose my belief on you or vice versa. Logical contradictions are OK for the liberal.

Truth is incidental, and image is everything.

NEOORTHODOX VIEW

As we have already seen, in the neoorthodox view the Bible *becomes* the Word of God. It is a record of man's encounters with God and is a combination of divine truth and human error. It is an imperfect but unique book which God uses as a means to encounter man. The Bible becomes God's Word to a person as he or she experiences its reality in his or her life. I've already commented on this view in great detail earlier in this chapter, so I will continue with the next type.

LIMITED INERRANCY VIEW

Limited inerrancy holds that the Bible is the Word of God and the word of man. The parts which deal with salvation, faith, and practice are God's words. Those parts that speak to culture, science, and history are man's words. It is left to the individual to decide which are God's words and which are merely man's opinions.

At this point, John Murray makes an incisive statement:

> If human fallibility precludes an infallible Scripture, then by relentless logic it must be maintained that we cannot have any Scripture that is infallible and inerrant. All Scripture comes to us through human instrumentality. If such instrumentality involves fallibility, then such fallibility must attach to the whole of Scripture. For by what warrant can an immunity from error be maintained in the matter of "spiritual content" and not in the matter of historical or scientific fact? Is human infallibility suspended when "spiritual truth" is asserted, but not suspended in other less important matters?[1]

Well said! What this ultimately does is to make the mind of man take precedence over the Word of God. There's an old baseball story that goes something like this. Three umpires were asked how they made their calls of balls and strikes. The first answered, "I call them as they are." The second replied, "I call them as I see them." Whereupon the third said, "They ain't nothing 'til I call them." It seems to me that they need to be called as they are.

THE WORD OF GOD VIEW

I believe the Bible is the Word of God. God was the author of the whole Bible. It was inspired by him but written through human agents. It is true in every area in which it speaks regardless of our human response to it.

In the Southern Baptist denomination of which I am a part, there has been a great battle over the Word of God. The battle began and continues to revolve around the question of the authority of the Bible as the Word of the King. In my estimation, this is the vital question of the day and the underpinning issue in spiritual authority.

In understanding the battle lines of spiritual authority, I want to mention the concept of "inerrancy." This term simply means that the Bible is without error as God originally gave it. John Wesley believed in inerrancy. He said, "If there be any mistakes in the Bible there may as well be a thousand. If there be one falsehood in that book it did not come from the God of truth."

It is not my purpose in this book to prove or disprove the inerrancy of the Bible. I have settled that matter long ago in my heart. If you haven't, I ask that you strongly consider doing that as well. Other authors have dealt with fervent scholarship on the subject of the inerrancy of God's Word. If you have any doubts in this regard, I encourage you to visit a good Christian bookstore and learn about this foundational truth. One book I would recommend is *The Inspiration and Authority of the Bible* by B. B. Warfield, who said, "The Bible is the Word of God in such a way that when the Bible speaks, God speaks."

My purpose here is to discuss the corresponding authority of the Word of God that is the Word of our King.

We can never speak with authority, preach with authority, witness with authority, live with authority, or serve with authority until we get under the authority of the Word of God. It is an issue of basic truth. Until you deal with truth and stand upon it, you will have no real authority. We cannot walk with authority unless we're walking on solid ground. There must be more than eggshells beneath our spiritual feet.

GOD'S FAVORITE NAME FOR THE BIBLE

God's favorite name for the Bible is the *Word of God*. The Bible records these words, "The Lord said" or "The Lord spoke" or "the word of the Lord" over three thousand times in the Old Testament alone! The Bible is the Word of God lest we have any doubt. God put his words into the mouths and on the pages of man for our understanding, edification, instruction, and his glory. Think on a few of these verses that call such revelation the Word of God:

"Every *word of God* is pure: he is a shield unto them that put their trust in him" (Prov. 30:5).

"And it came to pass, that, as the people pressed upon him to hear the *word of God,* he stood by the lake of Gennesaret" (Luke 5:1).

"But he said, Yea rather, blessed are they that hear the *word of God,* and keep it" (Luke 11:28).

"And when they had prayed, the place was shaken where they were assembled together; and they were all filled with the Holy Ghost, and they spake the *word of God* with boldness" (Acts 4:31).

"But the *word of God* grew and multiplied" (Acts 12:24).

"So then faith cometh by hearing, and hearing by the *word of God*" (Rom. 10:17).

"And take the helmet of salvation, and the sword of the Spirit, which is the *word of God*" (Eph. 6:17).

"Whereof I am made a minister, according to the dispensation of God which is given to me for you, to fulfil the *word of God*" (Col. 1:25).

"For this cause also thank we God without ceasing, because, when ye received the *word of God* which ye heard of us, ye received it not as the word of men, but as it is in truth, the *word of God,* which effectually worketh also in you that believe" (1 Thess. 2:13).

"For it is sanctified by the *word of God* and prayer" (1 Tim. 4:5).

"For the *word of God* is quick, and powerful, and sharper than any two-edged sword, piercing even to the dividing asunder of soul and spirit, and of the joints and marrow, and is a discerner of the thoughts and intents of the heart" (Heb. 4:12).

"Through faith we understand that the worlds were framed by the *word of God,* so that things which are seen were not made of things which do appear" (Heb. 11:3–4).

"For this they willingly are ignorant of, that by the *word of God* the heavens were of old, and the earth standing out of the water and in the water" (2 Pet. 3:5).

"And I saw thrones, and they sat upon them, and judgment was given unto them: and I saw the souls of them that were beheaded for the witness of Jesus, and for the *word of God,* and which had not worshipped the beast, neither his image, neither had received his mark upon their foreheads, or in their hands; and they lived and reigned with Christ a thousand years" (Rev. 20:4).

That God calls the Bible the Word of God over and over again is interesting to me. I have noticed that the more liberal a person becomes in his theology, the less he refers to the Bible as the Word of God. Instead, he begins to use such phrases as "the biblical materials," "the record of God's revelation," or "the Pauline epistles." All of these phrases may be legitimate ways of speaking of the Bible, yet over and over again the Bible speaks of itself by divine inspiration as the *Word of God.*

Here are some Kingdom Authority principles that flow from the concept that the Bible is indeed the Word of God.

THE ABSOLUTE PERFECTION OF THE WORD OF GOD

If the Bible is indeed God's Word, then it must be perfect! "All scripture is given by inspiration of God, and is profitable for doctrine, for reproof, for correction, for instruction in righteousness: that the man of God may be perfect, thoroughly furnished unto all good works" (2 Tim. 3:16–17). *The God of truth cannot inspire error.*

God breathed out the Scriptures. The adjective used in the first part of 2 Timothy to describe how the Scriptures were given is *theopneustos,* which is a combination of two other Greek words: *theos* which means "God" and *pneo* which means "breathe." Logic tells us, therefore, that if *God breathed the words, then they must be absolutely perfect.* Psalm 19:7 says, "The law of the LORD is perfect, converting the soul: the testimony of the LORD is sure, making wise the simple." His Word is perfect. Jesus said the Scripture cannot be broken. How can foolish men think they can break what cannot be broken? The Bible is nothing less than revelation that comes from the transcendent, personal God. Take away inerrancy, and all that's left is human opinion.

Human penmanship does not make the Bible any less the Word of God than Jesus is any less the Son of God because he was born of a human woman named Mary. The same Holy Spirit who protected the Lord Jesus from defilement in his humanity is the same Holy Spirit who kept the human writers of Scripture from including error in what they wrote. Proverbs 30:5 tells us that every word of the Bible is pure.

Jesus said, "Man shall not live by bread alone, but by every word that proceedeth out of the mouth of God" (Matt. 4:4). The biblical writers weren't merely inspired authors. They were recorders of the inspired, perfect Word of God that came out of the mouth of God. The *breath* of God became the *Word* of God.

Paul said, "For what man knoweth the things of a man, save the spirit of man which is in him? even so the things of God knoweth no man, but the Spirit of God. Now we have received, not the spirit of the world, but the spirit which is of God; that we might know the things that are freely given to us of God. Which things also we speak, not in the words which man's wisdom teacheth, but which the Holy Ghost teacheth; comparing spiritual things with spiritual" (1 Cor. 2:11–13).

Peter affirmed this position when he said, "Knowing this first, that no prophecy of the scripture is of any private interpretation. For the prophecy came not in old time by the will of man: but holy men of God spake *as they were* moved by the Holy Ghost" (2 Pet. 1:20–21). The biblical writers knew from whom their words came. They knew it wasn't of their own accord, but of divine anointing. Let me put it simply—God cannot err. The Bible is the Word of God; therefore, the Bible cannot err.

THE WONDERFUL CHARACTER OF THE WORD OF GOD

God has not only called *his Book* the Word of God, but God has also called *his Son* the Word of God. John 1:1–3 says, "In the beginning was the Word, and the Word was with God, and the Word was God. The same was in the beginning with God. All things were made by him; and without him was not anything made that was made." Verse 14 of the same chapter says, "And the Word was made flesh, and dwelt among us, (and we beheld his glory, the glory as of the only begotten of the Father,) full of grace and truth." Revelation 19:13 says, "And his name is called The Word of God."

The Holy Spirit inspired the writers to call both Jesus and the Bible the Word of God. This means that the character of the Bible and the character of Jesus are inseparably linked together. If you will read the Bible from cover to cover, you will find that the *written* Word presents unerringly the *living* Word. And the living Word believed the written Word. There is a beautiful, miraculous connection.

BOTH ARE SIMILAR IN CONCEPTION.

Written Word

2 Timothy 3:16—"All scripture is given by inspiration of God, and is profitable for doctrine, for reproof, for correction, for instruction in righteousness."

Living Word

John 1:14—"And the Word was made flesh, and dwelt among us, (and we beheld his glory, the glory as of the only begotten of the Father,) full of grace and truth."

BOTH ARE SIMILAR IN CONTINUATION.

Written Word

Isaiah 40:8—"The grass withereth, and the flower fadeth: but the word of our God shall stand for ever."

Living Word

Hebrews 13:8—"Jesus Christ the same yesterday, and to day, and for ever."

BOTH ARE SIMILAR IN CREATIVITY.

Written Word

Hebrews 11:3—"Through faith we understand that the worlds were framed by the word of God, so that things which are seen were not made of things which do appear."

Living Word

Colossians 1:16—"For by him were all things created, that are in heaven, and that are in earth, visible and invisible, whether they be thrones, or dominions, or principalities, or powers: all things were created by him, and for him."

BOTH ARE SIMILAR IN CONVERSION.

Written Word

1 Peter 1:23–24—"Being born again, not of corruptible seed, but of incorruptible, by the word of God, which liveth and abideth for ever. For all flesh is as grass, and all the glory of man as the flower of grass. The grass withereth, and the flower thereof falleth away."

Living Word

Ephesians 1:7—"In whom we have redemption through his blood, the forgiveness of sins, according to the riches of his grace."

BOTH ARE SIMILAR IN CLEANSING.

Written Word

John 15:3—"Now ye are clean through the word which I have spoken unto you."

Living Word

1 John 1:9—"If we confess our sins, he is faithful and just to forgive us our sins, and to cleanse us from all unrighteousness."

Both are similar in condemnation.

Written Word

John 12:48—"He that rejecteth me, and receiveth not my words, hath one that judgeth him: the word that I have spoken, the same shall judge him in the last day."

Living Word

John 5:22—"For the Father judgeth no man, but hath committed all judgment unto the Son."

The Bible is as spotless in character as is the Lord Jesus. One would search in vain to find a flaw in the character of God's Word because it is just that—God's Word.

God's Word can have no rebuttal when it is properly interpreted. There are those who say that our faith is to be in Jesus, not in some inerrant book. But if we take a lesser view of the Bible, *we're making less of Jesus, as well,* by disbelieving his testimony. Jesus held the Word of God in the highest place of honor, and so must we. The servant's view of the Bible must be the same as his Lord's.

It is clear that Jesus, who is both our authority and role model, believed in the inerrancy and the authority of the Word of God. That Jesus regarded the Scriptures as inerrant is recognized by most scholars of every theological persuasion. How can we logically call Jesus Lord and reject his view of Scripture?

- Luke 24:25–27—"Then he [Jesus] said unto them, O fools, and slow of heart to believe all that the prophets have spoken: Ought not Christ to have suffered these things, and to enter into his glory? And beginning at Moses and all the prophets, he expounded unto them in all the scriptures the things concerning himself."
- John 5:39–47—"Search the scriptures; for in them ye think ye have eternal life: and they are they which testify of me. And ye will not come to me, that ye might have life. I receive not honour from men. But I know you, that ye have not the love of God

in you. I am come in my Father's name, and ye receive me not: if another shall come in his own name, him ye will receive. How can ye believe, which receive honour one of another, and seek not the honour that cometh from God only? Do not think that I will accuse you to the Father: there is one that accuseth you, even Moses, in whom ye trust. For had ye believed Moses, ye would have believed me: for he wrote of me. But if ye believe not his writings, how shall ye believe my words?"

- John 10:35—"If he called them gods, unto whom the word of God came, and the scripture cannot be broken; say ye of him, whom the Father hath sanctified, and sent into the world, Thou blasphemest; because I said, I am the Son of God?"

- Matthew 4:4—"But he [Jesus] answered and said, It is written, Man shall not live by bread alone, but by every word that proceedeth out of the mouth of God."

- Matthew 5:18—"For verily I say unto you, Till heaven and earth pass, one jot or one tittle shall in no wise pass from the law, till all be fulfilled."

THE AWESOME POWER OF THE WORD OF GOD

And would we not expect the Word of God to pulsate with power? In 1 Thessalonians 2:13, Paul said, "For this cause also thank we God without ceasing, because, when ye received the word of God which ye heard of us, ye received it not as the word of men, but as it is in truth, the word of God, which effectually worketh also in you that believe."

Because the Bible is the Word of God, it works effectually. We are . . .

Convicted by the word. Hebrews 4:12 says, "For the word of God is quick, and powerful, and sharper than any two-edged sword, piercing even to the dividing asunder of soul and spirit, and of the joints and marrow, and is a discerner of the thoughts and intents of the heart." There are no secrets that can be hidden from the Lord, who will use his sword to convict us of our waywardness and sin. B. C. Forbes said this about truth: "The truth doesn't hurt unless it ought to." The Word of God is a two-edged sword that God uses to protect us and to penetrate us.

Converted by the Word. First Peter 1:23 says, "Being born again, not of corruptible seed, but of incorruptible, by the word of God, which liveth and abideth for ever." We are born again in Christ who is the Word and promised the gift of eternal life through him.

Cleansed by the Word. John 15:3 says, "Now ye are clean through the word which I have spoken unto you." We've been purchased and washed clean of all our sins in the blood of our Savior Jesus Christ, who is the Word of God.

Controlled by the Word. Second Timothy 3:16–17 teaches, "All scripture is given by inspiration of God, and is profitable for doctrine, for reproof, for correction, for instruction in righteousness: that the man of God may be perfect, thoroughly furnished unto all good works." God's Word is a useful tool for us. It is a tool that guides us daily and eternally presents us complete before Christ.

Confirmed by the Word. John 5:24 says, "Verily, verily, I say unto you, He that heareth my word, and believeth on him that sent me, hath everlasting life, and shall not come into condemnation; but is passed from death unto life." It is the Word of God that keeps us from being a doubting Christian and allows us to be a shouting Christian.

Because of the Bible's absolute perfection, wonderful character, and awesome power, we cannot legitimately refuse it, deny it, distort it, or dilute it. We must bow before it.

In 1949, when Billy Graham was a very young man, he harbored the same doubts about the Bible that many young people have. When he stood up to preach, there was a lack of power. He knew an intellectual battle was waging in his mind over the authority of God's Word. That year God allowed him to spend some time in the mountains outside Los Angeles. There he wrestled with God and with himself. He said, "In desperation, I surrendered my will to the living God revealed in the Scripture. I knelt before the open Bible and said, 'Lord, many things in this book I do not understand, but thou hast said the just shall live by faith. All I have, I have received by faith. Here and now by faith, I accept the Bible as thy Word, I take it all, I take it without reservations. Where there are things I cannot understand, I will reserve judgment until I receive more light. If this pleases thee, give me authority as I proclaim thy word, and through that authority convict me of sin and turn sinners to the Savior.'"

Within six weeks of that prayer, Billy Graham preached the great Los Angeles crusade where thousands were swept into the kingdom of God. His ministry caught on fire for the Lord—making a global impact for the Savior! Now, he recognized that he didn't have to prove the Bible was true. He had settled it in his mind, and that faith impacted his preaching and the men and women who were saved as a result. Now he had a quick, powerful weapon in his hand—a two-edged sword that could pierce the heart of people. He had a flame with which to melt away the unbelief of people, a hammer to break up the stony covering of hearts. All this, Billy Graham says, is why, to this day, he frequently begins sentences with the phrase, "The Bible says. . . ."

Jesus knew this when he faced the great temptation in the wilderness as recorded in Matthew 4:1–11. Satan faced Jesus in that desert battle and fired at him his best artillery. Jesus relied not on reason or emotion to fight back; he simply unleashed the power of the Word. Jesus knew he was under the authority of the Word of God. Satan could only retreat.

Do you claim to believe every word of the Bible? Let me ask another question. Do you believe every word of the news on television? Many will answer respectively, "Yes," and "No." However, many spend more time with the latter than the former. They affirm the Bible is a treasure chest and the media is a junkyard—and then choose to spend their time in the junkyard!

What is the bottom line? Clearly, we must affirm that when the Bible speaks, we have the Word of heaven's King. True authority flows from this!

In order for Satan to take dominion from Adam, he had to plant a doubt concerning the Word of the King. "Yea, hath God said . . . ?" (Gen. 3:1). The last Adam came to affirm the Word of God, saying, "Yea,

God hath said!" "He hath said . . . so that we may boldly say . . ." (Heb. 3:5–6). What gives the Word of God authority is that it is the Word of God! A check has no authority of its own; the name attached to it gives it its value. God's promises are checks that will be cashed by heaven's bank. Thank God, we have a signed checkbook if we would only realize it. We don't have to get rich. We are already rich.

CHAPTER 10

THE AUTHORITY OF
THE HOLY SPIRIT

Nothing is settled until the matter of authority is settled. The church
that does not operate with Kingdom Authority is a farce, not a force.

Christians who do not live with Kingdom Authority are to be pitied.
They are indeed a disgrace to grace. Their lives defeat the purpose and
dishonor the glory of their sovereign Lord. A Christian without authority is a laughingstock to demons and an alibi for sinners to use in refusing the gospel.

I will remind you one more time that God wants you to live with
Kingdom Authority over the world, the flesh, and the devil. And again I
remind you that in order to be *over* those things that God has put *under*
you, you must remain *under* those things that God has set *over* you. This
includes the lordship of Christ, the authority of the holy Scriptures, and
the *authority of the Holy Spirit.* Paul tells of awesome authority exercised by the Holy Spirit:

> There is therefore now no condemnation to them which
> are in Christ Jesus, who walk not after the flesh, but after the
> Spirit. For the law of the Spirit of life in Christ Jesus hath
> made me free from the law of sin and death. For what the law

could not do, in that it was weak through the flesh, God sending his own Son in the likeness of sinful flesh, and for sin, condemned sin in the flesh: that the righteousness of the law
might be fulfilled in us, who walk not after the flesh, but after
the Spirit (Rom. 8:1–4).

Do you think of the Holy Spirit as having authority? Sound theology
teaches us that he is the Advocate sent from the Father to represent Jesus
here on earth. Jesus has given to the Holy Spirit his power of attorney.
Jesus said, "He shall not speak of himself. He is here to represent me."

There are some people, however, who have made an artificial distinction between the authority of the holy Scriptures and the authority
of the Holy Spirit. This is so foolish because it is the Holy Spirit who
inspired the Scriptures and he is the one who opens them to our heart.
Therefore, it is not the Spirit or the Word but the Spirit *and* the Word.
We're to worship our Lord in Spirit and in truth.

In order to understand what Paul declared in the Romans 8 passage,
we need to go back and get a running start. Romans 5 and 6 set the stage
for understanding the authority of the Holy Spirit.

A key verse is Romans 5:17 which says, "For if by one man's offence
death reigned by one; much more they which receive abundance of
grace and of the gift of righteousness shall reign in life by one, Jesus
Christ." The words *one* and *reign* and *much more* are vital to understanding Kingdom Authority.

What is this all about? This rich verse tells us of two kingdoms that
want to reign over us. And it tells us of one man for each kingdom who
heads up that kingdom. One man is Adam, and the other is Jesus. The
two kingdoms are the kingdoms of death and life. Each of us is identified with either Adam and the kingdom of death or Jesus and the kingdom of life.

The *much more* says, however, that when we have Kingdom
Authority with Jesus, we gain much more in him than we ever lost in
Adam. What did we receive from one man Adam and one man Jesus?

"For as by one man's disobedience many were made sinners, so by the obedience of one shall many be made righteous" (Rom. 5:19).

WHAT WE HAVE LOST IN ONE MAN—ADAM

Remember what we've already seen: that Adam sold himself into slavery and lost his God-given Kingdom Authority. Since the children of slaves are also slaves and we are sons and daughters of Adam, we are born into slavery. We all have our roots in Adam. There is no way you can deny your linkage with Adam. Simple logic says that if there had been no Adam, there would have been no you.

This might be a good time to remind ourselves that in the real sense we are not in the image of God. It was Adam who was made in the image of God, and we, being sons and daughters of Adam, are made in the image of Adam. Adam's children were in his likeness (see Gen. 5:3). If you think we're the image of God, look around and ask yourself—is God really in this shape? The truth of the matter is that the image of God has been marred and defaced. None of us has ever yet seen a person who is truly in the image of God. One day, of course, we will, when that image is restored in glory.

Suppose you had never seen a train and then you see a train wreck. Have you seen a train now? What you've really seen is not a train but a train wreck. The people around us are not men and women as God had intended. They are really derailed wrecks on earth's tracks.

In Adam We Inherit Weakness Rather than Power. "For when we were *yet without strength,* in due time Christ died for the ungodly" (Rom. 5:6). "Without strength" is more than physical weakness. It is primarily spiritual weakness. It means that we do not have the power to be what God made us to be. God made us for a purpose. We have not done what we were made to do because we were without strength to do it. We are free to do as we want but not free to do as we ought.

And the truth of the matter is that we're really not even free to do what we want.

In Adam We Inherit Wickedness Rather than Godliness. "For when we were yet without strength, in due time Christ died for the *ungodly*" (Rom. 5:6). What were we created to be? Godly! God made us to be like him—in his image. Being unlike God is really the problem. So many sit in churches and do not understand that they're sinners. The reason for this is that they have failed to evaluate themselves by God's standard, which is his glory.

Let me give you a definition of sin. "For all have sinned, and come short of the glory of God" (Rom. 3:23). Fools measure themselves by themselves. Even worse, we may measure ourselves by someone inferior to us. We lie down in the gutter and stretch ourselves out by some old sinner for a measurement. We have the wrong standard. Sin is the gap between man and the glory of God.

I heard of two brothers who were lasciviously wicked. One brother died and the other said to a pastor, "I will give you $500 if you will preach my brother's funeral and call him a saint." The pastor said, "You have a deal." The time for the funeral came. The pastor said, "The man in this casket is a liar, a drunkard, a thief, and a pervert, but compared to his brother, he is a saint." Indeed, we can look good by comparison until we measure by the "glory of God."

In Adam We Inherit Wrath Rather than Approval. "Much more then, being now justified by his blood, we shall be saved from wrath through him" (Rom. 5:9). Because of what we are, we're headed to where we're headed without Christ—to eternal hell. The wrath of God is politically incorrect today, but the Bible does not teach reincarnation, universalism, or annihilation. The Bible says that people without God are headed for judgment.

In Adam We Inherit Warfare Rather than Peace. "For if, when we were *enemies*, we were reconciled to God by the death of his Son, much more, being reconciled, we shall be saved by his life" (Rom. 5:10). Sin is really high treason against heaven's king. It is a clenched fist in the face of Almighty God. Jesus clearly taught this. "He that is not with me is against me; and he that gathereth not with me scattereth abroad" (Matt. 12:30). It is clear—we were enemies.

This poses, therefore, a question: Is God just to let us inherit the nature of Adam? Should we be condemned because of one man's disobedience? Indeed, not only is God just, but thank God, wise and gracious that he allows it to be so.

In the first place, if you had been tested the same way Adam was, the result would have been the same. For another matter, forget about Adam's sin and talk about yours. You have already sinned. You know that you're guilty before God, apart from Adam. But here's the wonderful part: God, in condemning the race through one man, is *also able to save the race through one man.* Be grateful for the one-man salvation!

WHAT WE HAVE GAINED IN THE ONE MAN—JESUS

"For as by one man's disobedience many were made sinners, so by the obedience of one shall many be made righteous" (Rom. 5:19). Remember that it was Jesus who was obedient unto death. He paid the sin debt in full. He satisfied God's justice and recovered Adam's lost estate.

Jesus Gave Us the "Much More" of Our Justification. *"Much more then, being now justified by his blood,* we shall be saved from wrath through him" (Rom. 5:9). Remember that before Adam fell, he was *merely innocent.* A redeemed sinner is totally justified. There is a great difference. Justice, mercy, and grace are blended at Calvary.

- Justice is God giving us what we deserve. If we get justice we go to hell.
- Mercy is God not giving us what we deserve. Thank God that we have escaped hell.
- *Grace is God giving us what we don't deserve.* That is the righteousness of God that comes with justification.

Joyce and I were witnessing to a waitress. Her heart was broken. She was in tears. We had not finished our meal before her quitting time, so she left the meal check on our table. When I looked at it, I saw that she had overcharged us. I did not want to tell the manager because of the trouble that was already in her heart. I was willing to pay the bill with the unfair overcharge, but here was the problem. The restaurant would not take a credit card, and I was limited on cash. I did have enough money to pay the overcharge but not enough to leave a tip. Here's the way we handled it.

I said, "Joyce, you stay here so they'll know we're not skipping out without paying the bill. I'll go home and get some more money so we can not only pay the overcharge but leave a tip." That's what we did. To this day the waitress knows nothing about it. Justice said I should not have paid the bill. Mercy said pay the bill so she would not suffer even more. Grace said go home and get a tip for the person who had over-charged us.

When my sins were placed on Jesus, God's justice was satisfied. When I was saved from wrath, God's mercy was shown. But when I was justified, God's grace was given.

Jesus Gave Us the "Much More" of Our Reconciliation. "For if, when we were enemies, we were reconciled to God by the death of his Son, *much more, being reconciled,* we shall be saved by his life" (Rom. 5:10). Jesus gave himself for us so he might indeed give himself to us. Now it is not God who is reconciled. The Bible never says that God is reconciled. He doesn't need to be. We are the ones who are reconciled. We now have a fellowship that Adam could never have known. While God walked with Adam in the garden, Jesus indwells us, never to leave us.

Jesus Gave Us the "Much More" of Our Regeneration. "But not as the offence, so also is the free gift. For if through the offence of one many be dead, *much more the grace of God,* and the gift by grace, which is by one man, Jesus Christ, hath abounded unto many" (Rom. 5:15). Remember that Adam had *natural* life, but we have *supernatural* life. It is the "much more" of his grace.

Adam had life on one plane, but we have the "much more" of abundant life. "The thief cometh not, but for to steal, and to kill, and to destroy: I am come that they might have life, and that they might have it more abundantly" (John 10:10). Indeed, I had rather live in Romans 5 than in the Garden of Eden.

Jesus Gave Us the "Much More" of Our Righteousness. "For if by one man's offence death reigned by one; *much more they which receive abundance of grace and of the gift of righteousness* shall reign in life by one, Jesus Christ" (Rom. 5:17). I remind you one more time that Adam, before he fell, was merely innocent. The twice-born child of God is positively righteous. Adam could have sin placed on his account, but that can never be done to us. "Blessed is the man to whom the Lord will not impute sin" (Rom. 4:8). Again I say, I had rather live in Romans 5 as a redeemed sinner than in the Garden of Eden as an innocent man!

Jesus Gave Us the "Much More" of Our Reigning. "Moreover the law entered, that the offence might abound. But where sin abounded, grace did much more abound: that as sin hath reigned unto death, even so might grace reign through righteousness unto eternal life by Jesus Christ our Lord" (Rom. 5:20–21). Now we're getting back to Kingdom Authority. Remember that Adam had an earthly dominion, and he lost it. We now have a kingdom of grace that can never be taken away. Adam was the head of the old creation, but we will rule and reign with Jesus for all eternity in a new creation. Not only that, we "reign in life" now (see Rom. 5:17).

Are you getting the thought? We gained *"much more"* in Christ than we ever lost in Adam. Our redemption is stronger at the place of repair than it was before it was ever broken. We were in Adam by our first birth, but we are in Jesus by our new birth.

WHAT SHALL WE SAY THEN?

Paul continues this incredible discussion in Romans 6 by asking a pertinent question. "What shall we say then? Shall we continue in sin, that grace may abound?" (Rom. 6:1). He then tells us how the Holy Spirit of God establishes Kingdom Authority in a vital way in our lives. This dynamic chapter hinges on three key words: "know" (v. 6), "reckon" (v. 11), and "yield" (v. 13).

THERE IS A MATTER OF FACT TO KNOW ABOUT

"Knowing this, that our old man is crucified with him, that the body of sin might be destroyed, that henceforth we should not serve sin" (Rom. 6:6). There's something we're to know with our mind. We are to know that our old man has been crucified with Christ. We have become one with him because he chose to become one with us. Substitution says he died for me, and that deals with sin's penalty. Identification says that I died with him, and that deals with sin's power. His death had my name on it. Amen!

Here's the great truth—when a man dies, the law has no more demand on him. Any impending criminal charges are automatically dropped. Also, if he is a slave, his master's power has no more effect on him. That relationship is terminated. The old master cannot tell him when to go to bed, when to get up, what to eat, or what he must do. Death has changed all of that. This is a *FACT.*

THERE IS A MATTER OF FAITH TO RECKON ON

"Likewise reckon ye also yourselves to be dead indeed unto sin, but alive unto God through Jesus Christ our Lord" (Rom. 6:11). Now, there's something we're to reckon with our heart.

The word *reckon* really is a bookkeeping term. It deals not primarily with feelings but with fact. It is something you can bank on. Reckoning is not closing your eyes and pretending something is true. It is not wishing it is true. It is knowing it is true and then calculating on what you know to be true.

You're reckoned in order to be saved from the penalty of sin. You trusted what Jesus did for you. What you need to understand is that you can also reckon and be saved from the power of sin. Because you died with Christ, the devil can make no demand on you. Because Christ lives in you, every demand upon your life is really a demand upon the life of Jesus Christ in you. Don't just know it as a fact. Bank on it!

THERE IS A MATTER OF FUNCTION TO YIELD TO

"*Let not sin* therefore reign in your mortal body, that ye should obey it in the lusts thereof. *Neither yield* ye your members as instruments of unrighteousness unto sin: but *yield yourselves* unto God, as those that are alive from the dead, and your members as instruments of righteousness unto God. For sin shall not have dominion over you: for ye are not under the law, but under grace" (Rom. 6:12–14).

Now the third word comes into play. It is the word *yield*. We are to yield to the Spirit of God. That's where the authority of the Holy Spirit comes in. We have Kingdom Authority. We are to know it, believe it, and act on it.

Paul says in verse 12, "Let not sin therefore reign." This means that you don't have to let sin reign in your life. You have been delivered. But in order to accomplish this you *must yield* to the authority of the Spirit in your life. There is a willing dethronement of sin and Satan and the enthronement of Jesus Christ. The word *yield* simply means to place yourself *under authority*. At the moment of yielding, Kingdom Authority takes over. "Where the Spirit of the Lord is, there is liberty." It is somewhat like the power steering in your car. When you give direction to the steering wheel the power takes over, but it waits on your decision.

LEARNING TO YIELD TO THE HOLY SPIRIT

Let me give you a few suggestions about yielding to the Holy Spirit. Remember that his guidance is promised in the Gospels by Jesus himself. "Howbeit when he, the Spirit of truth, is come, he will guide you into all truth: for he shall not speak of himself; but whatsoever he shall hear, *that* shall he speak: and he will show you things to come" (John 16:13).

Also his guidance is shown in the Book of Acts. "While Peter thought on the vision, the Spirit said unto him, Behold, three men seek thee" (Acts 10:19). "After they were come to Mysia, they assayed to go into Bithynia: but the Spirit suffered them not" (Acts 16:7). And in his Epistle to the Romans, Paul makes clear that the Spirit of God leads the people of God. "For as many as are led by the Spirit of God, they are the sons of God" (Rom. 8:14).

How can we tell, however, if it is the Spirit of God or some other voice? How can we assure ourselves that the Spirit is leading rather than autosuggestion or human impression? Many foolish and hurtful things have been done by people who claim to have been led by the Spirit of God or some "inner light."

One of the keys that I've found is to be aware of anything that disturbs our peace with God. Colossians 3:15 says, "Let the peace of God rule in your hearts." The Greek word translated as *rule* is a verb form of the word for a judge or a referee in an athletic game. I can tell when I'm "out of bounds" because the Holy Spirit will blow the whistle. If you are walking in the Spirit, you will hear the whistle.

There is authority everywhere, and we must yield. I was with some friends at a restaurant. We wanted to move some tables together so we could sit together. The waitress said, "You can't do that." To me it was obvious that we could and for practical purposes should. Had I been a manager in the restaurant, not only would I have encouraged it; I would have seen that it was done.

At the time of this event, I was serving as president of the Southern Baptist Convention—the world's largest evangelical denomination. Here's a waitress telling us that we could not do a very reasonable thing. My first impression was to just do it anyway, and so I started to move the tables. At that moment the Holy Spirit blew a whistle and said, "Adrian, you're out of bounds. She is in authority here." Indeed she was. I submitted, and I am glad that I did.

I have found that to yield to him in small things, everyday things, practical things makes it so much easier to yield in times of crisis. Oh, there is *so much more* in Jesus! We need to know it, reckon on it, and yield to it. Then, the mighty Spirit of God releases the awesome power of Kingdom Authority, and we can shout that "the law of the Spirit of life in Christ Jesus hath made me free from the law of sin and death" (Rom. 8:2)!

PART IV

Learning the Places of Kingdom Authority

CHAPTER 11

IN THE HOME LIFE

For the husband is the head of the wife,
even as Christ is the head of the church:
and he is the saviour of the body.
—EPHESIANS 5:23

You would have thought World War III had just begun. The media elite were aghast! The Southern Baptist Convention (SBC) in its annual convention had affirmed a statement of belief concerning the relationship between men and women that brought a hailstorm of criticism and sent the mainstream media into orbit. It was a front-page story in the *New York Times*. Southern Baptist males were made to look like Neanderthals, and the convention was portrayed as a relic from the past. Just what was this politically incorrect statement? Here is the wording of the revised section of the SBC's Statement of the Baptist Faith and Message:

> God has ordained the family as the foundational institution of human society. It is composed of persons related to one another by marriage, blood, or adoption.
> Marriage is the uniting of one man and one woman in covenant commitment for a lifetime. It is God's unique gift to

reveal the union between Christ and His church and to provide for the man and the woman in marriage the framework for intimate companionship, the channel of sexual expression according to biblical standards, and the means for procreation of the human race.

The husband and wife are of equal worth before God, since both are created in God's image. The marriage relationship models the way God relates to His people. A husband is to love his wife as Christ loved the church. He has the God-given responsibility to provide for, to protect, and to lead his family. A wife is to submit herself graciously to the servant leadership of her husband even as the church willingly submits to the headship of Christ. She, being in the image of God as is her husband and thus equal to him, has the God-given responsibility to respect her husband and to serve as his helper in managing the household and nurturing the next generation.

Children, from the moment of conception, are a blessing and heritage from the Lord. Parents are to demonstrate to their children God's pattern for marriage. Parents are to teach their children spiritual and moral values and to lead them, through consistent lifestyle example and loving discipline, to make choices based on biblical truth. Children are to honor and obey their parents.

Bonnie Erbe, a columnist with Scripps-Howard News Services, was typical in her response. Here are a few choice quotes:

It's hard to see how anyone could espouse the view of marriage being considered by Southern Baptists. Southern Baptist (and other) women, unite. If ever there were a rallying cry for women of one faith to teach a lesson to their menfolk, it comes this week at the Southern Baptists' annual convention in (of all places) Salt Lake City.

The Baptist Faith and Message—the church's declaration of beliefs—was amended Tuesday at the convention to include a statement on marriage and family that reads, in part: "A husband . . . has the God-given responsibility to provide for, to protect and to lead his family," while "a wife is to submit graciously to the servant leadership of her husband even as the church willingly submits to the headship of Christ."

It goes on to say the wife has "the God-given responsibility to respect her husband and to serve as his 'helper' in managing her household and nurturing the next generation."

Southern Baptists are clearly not the only religious group to treat women in a subservient manner. And there probably are plenty of Southern Baptist women who fall for the idealized vision of a protective husband and a sheltered, home- and child-centered existence. But this amendment is so degrading and atavistic that it is hard to believe even a group of male devotees could suggest its approval in 1998.

Church leaders (all men, of course) say the amendment is necessary because challenges to the structure of the family over the last 50 years have come so fast and furiously as to threaten annihilation of the basic family unit. The amendment's purpose is to reject one-parent families, divorce, same-sex couples and everyone else who does not submit to modern warped interpretations of ancient Biblical Scriptures.

Well, that at least ought to set the stage for this chapter dealing with Kingdom Authority in the home life. Perhaps the home is the last place on earth that Satan wants to see Kingdom Authority exercised. It was the first home in Eden where mankind lost authority, and it is no wonder that all of the artillery of hell is leveled against today's home. The modern movement to deny sexual differences and God-assigned roles is a tool of Satan and may be the biggest threat to present-day society.

The thing to remember about the furor raised with reference to the SBC Statement of the Baptist Faith and Message is this—the statement comes straight out of the Word of God. For our discussion, we will focus on the following verses from Ephesians 5 and 6:

Wives, submit yourselves unto your own husbands, as unto the Lord. For the husband is the head of the wife, even as Christ is the head of the church: and he is the saviour of the body. Therefore as the church is subject unto Christ, so let the wives be to their own husbands in every thing.

Husbands, love your wives, even as Christ also loved the church, and gave himself for it; that he might sanctify and cleanse it with the washing of water by the word, that he might present it to himself a glorious church, not having spot, or wrinkle, or any such thing; but that it should be holy and without blemish. So ought men to love their wives as their own bodies. He that loveth his wife loveth himself.

For no man ever yet hated his own flesh; but nourisheth and cherisheth it, even as the Lord the church: for we are members of his body, of his flesh, and of his bones. For this cause shall a man leave his father and mother, and shall be joined unto his wife, and they two shall be one flesh.

This is a great mystery: but I speak concerning Christ and the church. Nevertheless let every one of you in particular so love his wife even as himself; and the wife *see* that she reverence her husband.

Children, obey your parents in the Lord: for this is right. Honour thy father and mother; which is the first commandment with promise; that it may be well with thee, and thou mayest live long on the earth. And, ye fathers, provoke not your children to wrath: but bring them up in the nurture and admonition of the Lord (Eph. 5:22–6:4).

THE LEADERSHIP ROLE OF THE HUSBAND/FATHER

The gifted writer Stu Weber has rightly said, "The problem in America is failure in the highest office in the land, that office being husband and father."

Ephesians 5:23 teaches that Christ is enthroned as the head of the church and has likewise placed the husband as the head of the family. First of all, let's see what the God-given assignments to the man are as the apostle Paul spells them out.

SERVANT LEADER

To be a servant *and* a leader is seen as an oxymoron in our modern society. Yet that is just what the Word of God teaches. When the Bible teaches that the husband should be the head of the home, it does not imply that he is a dictator or drill sergeant using the Bible as a club to thump the heads of his subjects. Rather, he is to be like Jesus, who has a cherishing, loving responsibility over the church, his bride. As Christ serves the church, so husbands should serve their homes. Headship, as we will learn, is about responsibility assumed, not about rights demanded.

The example is Jesus. As the sovereign Lord of the church, he leads by love. Ask yourself, "When did Jesus force me to do anything?" If you are honest, you will have to admit—never. Not one time did the Lord force your hand. Yet if I know my own heart, I would lay down my life for Jesus. Not because I fear him, but because I love him. He has won my submission.

The lordship of Christ is a supremacy that is gladly accepted by those who love him. Jesus does not need to be a dictator because he rules from a throne of love, and we respond in love. That leadership models what a husband needs to be—a servant leader.

Jesus taught many times that the way of authority is the path of a servant. Jesus speaks to this in Luke 9:46–50, 22:25–26; Matthew 18:1–5, 20:26–28; and Mark 9:33–37. In Luke 22:25–26, it is beautifully stated, "The kings of the Gentiles exercise lordship over them; and they that exercise authority upon them are called benefactors. But ye shall not be so: but he that is greatest among you, let him be as the younger; and he that is chief, as he that doth serve."

How do you find authority? Use the servant's entrance! The Lord Jesus was a leader who served. His agape love saw my need and took the resources of his life to meet that need.

In one of his last opportunities to model his leadership style during his earthly ministry, Jesus washed his disciples' feet. The Master and Lord said, "Ye call me Master and Lord: and ye say well; for so I am. If I then, your Lord and Master, have washed your feet; ye also ought to wash one another's feet. For I have given you an example, that ye should do as I have done to you" (John 13:13–15).

The way for a husband to be the head of his home is to wash his wife's feet by practical service. Husband, you are to serve in humility. Did you know that it is physically impossible to look down on the one whose feet you are washing? A country song says, "A woman wants a man she can look up to who won't look down on her."

Headship is not a *privilege demanded,* but a *responsibility assumed.* If a husband claims the title as head of the home, as well he should, then a wife has a proper expectation that her husband will meet her needs as she expects Christ to meet the needs of the church.

Does the wife accept an inferior role when the husband becomes the head? Does it mean that she is less than he is—to grovel at his feet? Certainly not. According to Galatians 3:28, "There is neither Jew nor Greek, there is neither bond nor free, there is neither male nor female: for ye are all one in Christ Jesus." The husband and wife are equals before God, but equality of worth is not sameness of function. God created male and female different at the very beginning. Why? God made us different that he might make us one.

The devil, under the guise of wanting us to see ourselves as equal, is trying to make us the same. Yet the Bible clearly teaches that God made them male and female. A man is a man. A woman is a woman. And God created men as masculine creatures and females as feminine creatures. We are to celebrate the difference, not discriminate against it. A woman is superior to a man at being a woman and a man is superior to a woman at being a man. Our society is trying to make women act like men and vice versa. How sad for the children who are being raised by creatures who are neither real men nor real women.

A home needs a head, and the Bible's designation of the husband in this role does not give the husband special privilege, much less the right of way to roll over his family in a dictatorship style. The man who does this may have a head-on collision with reality. That reminds me of a little poem:

> Here lies the body of Benjamin May,
> Who died defending the right of way.
> He was right, dead right, as he sped along,
> But just as dead as if he was wrong.

A husband who leads in love doesn't boast about his position as head of the home. The best leadership comes from the man who walks in the sandals of a servant.

Superiority and inferiority do not enter the equation of husband and wife. Let me provide a personal example. My wife is superior to me in many ways. She made much better grades than I made in school. When we were teens, she beat me in a church Better Speakers Tournament. She now handles all our finances with skill.

At this point, I want to borrow an illustration from David McLaughlin. He wisely says that in husband and wife relationships, partnership is not the best model. He says teamship is a better model. In partnership, there are two or more heads. How then are final decisions made? There are many ways but many opportunities for great conflict.

A team only has one head. For example, in the game of football, a quarterback (my old position) is the team leader. Why? Simply because the coach says so. This doesn't mean that the quarterback is the strongest, the fastest, or the most skilled. He may not be. Correspondingly, the man may not be the most competent. But that does not make the woman the head of the family. How does the team make decisions? The quarterback calls the play. On that same team with an average quarterback, there may be a stellar athlete who will go on to play professional football and make millions.

Again, marriage is very much like that. The husband is the quarterback because the Lord has said so. As an old quarterback and a husband with much experience, I know that it is wise to listen to the coach and consult with the team before calling a crucial play.

There is no way that the husband can escape the responsibility of leadership if he follows the biblical model. Responsibility is an awesome thing. Admiral Hyman Rickover, who spearheaded development of the atomic submarine, left us these incisive words:

> Responsibility is a unique concept. It can only reside in a single individual. You may share it with others, but your portion is not diminished. You may delegate it, but it is still with you. You may disclaim it, but you cannot divest yourself of it. If you do not recognize it or admit its presence, you cannot escape it. If responsibility is rightfully yours, not evasion, or ignorance, or passing the blame can shift the burden to someone else. Unless you can point your finger at the man who is responsible when something goes wrong, then you've never had anyone really responsible.

In the home, I remind you that it is the husband's responsibility to lead. He cannot dodge that responsibility. And who has said so? Almighty God!

I am convinced that today's major problem is not militant feminism or rebellious wives. Rather, it is husbands who are not doing what God has called them to do. The husband is the servant leader. He leads his family as Christ leads his church.

SACRIFICIAL LOVE

In John 15, one of the most beautiful passages in all of Scripture, we read about how much Jesus loved us. He said, "This is my commandment, That ye love one another, as I have loved you. Greater love hath no man than this, that a man lay down his life for his friends" (John 15:12–13).

This is the sacrificial love that lays the foundation for what Paul is speaking of in Ephesians 5:25, "Husbands, love your wives, even as Christ also loved the church, and gave himself for it." How am I to love my wife? As Christ loved the church and died for her. Sacrificial love is passionate, purifying, and protecting.

SACRIFICIAL LOVE IS PASSIONATE LOVE

On the surface, this love may show itself in the romance of hearts and music, but I'm talking about something far deeper and stronger than that. The passionate love shared between a husband and his wife is more than emotion-filled. It is commitment-driven. There is nothing too precious, apart from his relationship with God, that a man shouldn't be willing to give up for his wife.

I have been the pastor of Bellevue Baptist Church for more than a quarter of a century, but I wouldn't have to think twice if I were faced with a choice whether to give up this church or to give up my wife. The church is Jesus' bride, not mine. The church can get another pastor. I am Joyce's husband. She is my highest love on this earth apart from the Lord Jesus. Husband, what do you owe your wife? You owe her your life. Jesus gave up his life for the church. And I would do the same for Joyce because of my passionate love for her.

SACRIFICIAL LOVE IS PURIFYING LOVE

Continuing in Ephesians 5, Paul explains that Christ died for the church so "that he might sanctify and cleanse it with the washing of water by the word, that he might present it to himself a glorious church, not having spot, or wrinkle, or any such thing; but that it should be holy and without blemish" (vv. 26–27). Jesus' love is both passionate *and* purifying.

What does it mean for a husband to have a *purifying* love for his wife? As Jesus is prophet, priest, and pastor to the church, husbands should be interceding, teaching, and leading their wives into a more pure relationship with God. My chief assignment from God is to make my wife a more radiantly beautiful Christian—just as Jesus gave himself to make his bride, the church, glorious.

The husband is like a pastor in the home. He is to be a spiritual leader to whom his wife can turn when she has questions. First Corinthians 14:34–35 makes an interesting assertion: "Let your women keep silence in the churches: for it is not permitted unto them to speak; but they are commanded to be under obedience, as also saith the law. And if they will learn any thing, let them ask their husbands at home: for it is a shame for women to speak in the church."

When women have questions in church, they are supposed to save them and ask their husbands at home. Why? Because God has ordained the husband as the wife's spiritual head. This word doesn't mean that women are not allowed to utter a peep in church. And it doesn't mean that women cannot sing or pray in church. To put it in a larger context, God has put men in spiritual authority at church and in the home. Men are the voice of their home like Joshua of old who said, "As for me and my house, we will serve the LORD" (Josh. 24:15c).

Think about it for a moment—what would happen if the women in America saved their questions concerning the things of God for their husbands? As the situation is now, most of the husbands would not have the answers. They would have to learn them. It would nudge them in the direction of spiritual responsibility. What God really wants to do is to work on the husbands. If wives go to someone else to get their answers, it is almost as if the work God wants to do in the lives of their husbands is sidelined. God wants to work in and through men with a ministry of purifying love for their wives.

SACRIFICIAL LOVE IS PROTECTING LOVE

The husband's love should also be *protective*. Ephesians 5:28 tells husbands to love their wives as their own bodies. When a man doesn't care for himself physically, his health deteriorates. Sickness comes. Correspondingly, a home in which the wife is unprotected and uncared for soon becomes an unhealthy home.

First Peter 3:7 says that the husband is to give honor to the wife, "as unto the weaker vessel." *Weaker* does not mean *inferior.* Silk is weaker than denim. It's not inferior. It's more refined, more fragile, and more intrinsically beautiful. Gold is weaker than steel, but not inferior! God intends men of steel and women of gold. Gold should always be protected in a safe of steel. In the marriage relationship, God intended the wife to be like an ornament of gold.

A man has a God-given intrinsic drive to protect his wife. I'm not physically as strong as I once was, but if someone lays a hand on my wife, if I'm able, I will put him on the ground because God has given me an instinct to protect her. But not only to protect her *physically*. I also need to protect her *emotionally* and *spiritually*.

Husbands, did you know that in order for Satan to attack your family, he must come through you? From the beginning, God placed the husband as the sentinel of the garden to oversee and protect. In Matthew 12:29 we learn that no one can "enter into a strong man's house, and spoil his goods, except he first bind the strong man." If Satan can go through the husband, he can get at the family.

The husband has the responsibility and the authority to protect the home from demonic intruders and influences. Satan must come through him to get at the family. Satan hopes the husband will stay ignorant of this responsibility and authority.

Of course, the husband cannot override his wife's will if she willingly chooses to do evil. Also, if the husband fails, the wife may step into the gap and intercede for her family. But these facts do not free the husband from his responsibility to be a "strong man."

Such manhood is described in 1 Corinthians 16:13–14: "Watch ye, stand fast in the faith, quit you like men, be strong. Let all your things be done with charity."

He is to be vigilant—"watch ye."

He is to be faithful—"stand fast."

He is to be courageous—"quit you like men."

He is to be loving—"let all your things be done with charity."

No man is adequate for such a role without the incredible power of Kingdom Authority.

SACRIFICIAL LOVE IS PROVIDING LOVE

Ephesians 5:29 says, "For no man ever yet hated his own flesh; but nourisheth and cherisheth it, even as the Lord the church." The word *nourishing* means to feed and *cherishing* means to warm with body heat.

A wise man provides for his wife not only because he loves her but because he loves himself. When he is hungry, he wants to eat. When he is cold, he wants to be warmed. When the two were joined and became one flesh, the needs of one intimately became the needs of the other. The wife is a part of the husband. If he ignores her needs, he is hurting himself. To put it more bluntly, if the married man does not meet his wife's needs, he is committing spiritual and matrimonial suicide.

How does a husband provide for his wife's emotional needs? Praise her. Let her know in so many ways how valuable she is. This is crucial. Have you ever wondered why there are so many women in the work force today? Some need to work and my hat is off to them—my heart goes out to them, and my prayers are with them. But did you know many women work in order to get an emotional paycheck? Every payday, they are able to say, "I am worth something."

If husbands were affirming the invaluable worth of their wives and paying them an emotional paycheck out of their spiritual bank account, there would be more happy homes. It is the duty and responsibility of every husband to give his wife her due recognition.

Some husbands will simply praise their wives for their physical traits. That's fine, but don't forget to be wise. I heard about a husband whose wife asked him if her dress made her look fat. He said, "No. It's your hips that make you look fat." Not too smart! Be wise. Remember that physical beauty will fade. If that is all you praise, it may be a subtle threat to her.

The husband needs to search out those unique qualities of his wife that make her special—maybe it's her gentle and quiet spirit through which God affirms her radiant beauty. He should thank her for the little things she does, as well as the big things. He should praise her for her daily commitment as a wife and mother, for her gifts of serving and hospitality, for her prayer life, and everything else within his creative observation. He should meet her emotional needs every bit as much as her physical and spiritual needs.

Sometimes it's hard to figure out how to meet her emotional needs when you cannot figure out what she's communicating. Husbands must become better listeners.

Many women transmit emotionally while men tend to receive logically. Men need to become detectives at decoding and translating. Figure out what she means, not simply what she is saying. Men must listen, but above all, they must love. It may sound very simplistic, but love will cover a multitude of miscommunications (1 Pet. 4:8). Husbands must love, and it must be a providing love.

Let me list what I consider the seven basic emotional needs of a wife. I asked Joyce to read them, and she agreed, adding, "Be sure to practice them!" Here they are:

1. She needs the *confidence* that issues from your spiritual leadership.

2. She needs the *assurance* that she is meeting vital and satisfying needs in your life.

3. She needs the *joy* of knowing that she is cherished by you and that you delight in her as a person.

4. She needs the *peace* of knowing you understand her limitations and will lovingly cover and protect her in these areas.

5. She needs the intimate *fellowship* that comes with your attention and quality conversation with her.

6. She needs the *affirmation* that you are committed to her above all other persons.

7. She needs the *trust* that you will never willingly deceive her in any matter.

STEADFAST LOYALTY

No man can exercise Kingdom Authority in the home without the quality of steadfast loyalty. Returning to our passage from Ephesians 5 look closely at verses 30–33: "For we are members of his body, of his flesh, and of his bones. For this cause shall a man leave his father and mother, and shall be joined unto his wife, and they two shall be one flesh. This is a great mystery: but I speak concerning Christ and the church. Nevertheless let every one of you in particular so love his wife even as himself; and the wife see that she reverence her husband."

There is a great analogy in this passage between a man and his wife, and Christ and his church. Just as Eve was taken from the wounded side of Adam, the church has been taken from the wounded side of Christ and is his bride.

The marriage, therefore, should reflect and be modeled after the relationship of Christ and the church. Thank God for the steadfastness of Jesus to the church. I am so grateful to rest in his unqualified promise to me, "I will never leave thee, nor forsake thee" (Heb. 13:5).

May God have mercy upon our throwaway marriages in this generation. Where is the loyalty? Indeed, sometimes a woman is disloyal in her marriage, but primarily the problem is with the man. Surely, there will be problems in marriage. My bride and I have had plenty of them. But why let a wonderful marriage go down the tubes because of problems? There are no problems too big to solve—just people too small to solve them.

People who get divorced and those who are happily married have basically the same kinds of problems. The difference is in loyalty and commitment. Remember, it is not only *love that sustains marriage* but also *marriage that sustains love.*

According to the Word of God, the marriage relationship is a bond greater than that of parent and child, or child and parent: "Therefore shall a man leave his father and his mother, and shall cleave unto his wife: and they shall be one flesh" (Gen. 2:24). According to this verse, there is no higher commitment—not business, position, or service.

Yes, there is a price to pay for a marriage that lasts, but I can testify that it is well worth it. There is no such thing as "free love." Love is linked to loyalty, and it is not free—it costs. Kids today talk about "going all the way." The sad thing is that's exactly what they are *not doing.* They have not made a commitment to each other.

Sometimes a man may seek to get out of his marriage responsibility and headship with this excuse, "I owe it to myself to be happy." He thinks he has found another relationship that will make him happy. Rubbish! He owes it to himself to keep his commitment. He owes it to his wife to be loyal to his vows. He owes it to his children who did not ask to be fathered by him to give them stability. "Oh, the children will be happier if we separated rather than fuss." Why don't you ask them if they would?

Most of all, you owe it to Almighty God before whom you made a sacred vow to your wife, to love her, "until death do us part."

Besides all of that—love is not primarily a *feeling.* It is a *choice* that is initiated by a command, "Husbands, love your wives." Remember that behind every command of God is the omnipotent power of God to carry it out if we will depend on him. A man can choose to love his wife, and God will give him the power to do it. Choose to be lovingly loyal, and you will find Kingdom Authority flowing through you.

I have already dealt with the principle of submission for a wife in a former chapter. But I want to address a few more words directly to the wives who may be reading this.

Please model submission and femininity before your husband and children. Our society has been devastated with confusion over the meaning of true sexuality as God intended. The tragic result is more promiscuity, sexual abuse, homosexuality, divorce, and emotional disasters in the family.

God created the woman for a certain role. (I can hear the distant thunder as the storm clouds gather in the land of "political correctness.") Yet the earnest plea of my heart is for biblical manhood and womanhood.

This is not the bondage caricatured by so many, but instead it promises true freedom for the wife to be all that God intended her to be. The role of submission enables her to live as a queen with Kingdom Authority. If male and female are coequal in authority, the weaker vessel loses much and gains nothing.

She cannot have the special respect due to her. The mutual attraction of two complementary halves is gone. Two equal wills bring division, not unity. Satan will not give this point over easily, so he has made a last-ditch effort to come up with a concept called "mutual submission." Here is the way it is done.

First, let's begin with what God's Word says, "Submitting yourselves one to another in the fear of God. Wives, submit yourselves unto your own husbands, as unto the Lord" (Eph. 5:21–22). This view then adds this spin, "Of course, wives are to be subject to husbands, but the husband is also to be subject to the wife. It is mutual submission."

To say such, however, is to distort and subvert the meaning of Scripture. In a marriage there should be mutual respect, love, and helpfulness, but the principle of the husband's headship and the wife's submission remains.

Wayne Grudem has a definitive word concerning the Greek word *hypotasso* which is translated "be subject" or "submit to": "Although some have claimed that the word can mean 'be thoughtful and considerate; act in love' (toward another), there is no hard evidence to show that any first-century Greek speaker would have understood it in that way, for the term always implies a relationship of submission to an authority."[1]

Look at how this word is used elsewhere in the New Testament:

- Jesus is subject to the authority of his parents (Luke 2:51).
- Demons are subject to the disciples (Luke 10:17: clearly the meaning "act in love, be considerate" cannot fit here).
- Citizens are to be subject to government authorities (Rom. 13:1, 5; Titus 3:1; 1 Pet. 2:13).
- The universe is subject to Christ (1 Cor. 15:27; Eph. 1:22).
- Unseen powers are subject to Christ (1 Pet. 3:22).
- Christ is subject to God the Father (1 Cor. 15:28).
- Church members are to be subject to church leaders (1 Cor. 16:15–16; 1 Pet. 5:5).
- Wives are to be subject to husbands (Col. 3:18; Titus 2:5; 1 Pet. 3:5; compare Eph. 5:22, 24).
- The church is subject to Christ (Eph. 5:24).
- Servants are to be subject to masters (Titus 2:9; 1 Pet. 2:18).
- Christians are subject to God (Heb. 12:9; James 4:7).

Here is the point: None of these relationships is ever reversed. Husbands are never told to be subject (*hypotassō*) to wives, nor government to citizens, nor masters to servants, nor disciples to demons. Clearly parents are never told to be subject to their children! In fact the term *hypotassō* is used outside the New Testament to describe the submission and obedience of soldiers in an army to those of superior rank.

It is clear that *hypotassō* means to be subject to an authority.

Are parents supposed to submit to children and masters to servants because we are told to submit one to another? Hardly.

Actually, "one another" does not always mean "everyone to everyone." It may mean "some to others." Read what Grudem says further:

> For example in Revelation 6:4, "So that men should slay
> *one another*" means "so that some would kill others" (not "so

that every person would kill every other person," or "so that every person being killed would 'mutually' kill those who were killing them," which would make no sense!). In Galatians 6:2, "Bear *one another's* burdens" does not mean "everyone should exchange burdens with everyone else," but "some who are more able should help bear the burdens of others who are less able." In 1 Corinthians 11:33, "When you come together to eat, wait for *one another*" means "some who are ready early should wait for those who are late."[2]

Let me conclude with some words by my own dear wife:

God created woman from man with the *honored* position of being his helper or in other words—the executive vice-president of the "first corporation!" (Gen. 2:18). A number of Scriptures indicate that this is a "position of submission," though not of inferiority (Eph. 5:22–24; 1 Pet. 3:1,5; 1 Cor. 11:3 and others).

It was only when sin entered their lives that man began to treat the woman like a piece of property instead of giving her her "prized position." It is not her God-assigned role that is the problem; but the distortion caused by sin.

To prove that submission was a wonderful concept, Jesus became the ultimate illustration of its validity. He was completely submissive to his Father's will (John 8:28–29).

God the Son has a "position of submission" to God the Father yet being coequal and coeternal. Father and Son have equal worth but not sameness of function.

It is distressing to see some distorting the Scriptures that are meant for our good. Some would caricature those of us who believe in "biblical submission," as staying "barefoot, pregnant, and in the kitchen." But I personally have found fulfillment as a student, a teacher of God's Word, a leader of women and children, and someone who has been concerned for the *total program of the church.* In addition, going barefoot is delightful; being pregnant has been among the highest of privileges; and proper nutrition is among the most needed skills of our day.

Some who call themselves evangelical feminists and like-minded men attempt to redefine historically accepted terms; give strained interpretations, and in some cases actually twist the Word of God to say the opposite of its true meaning. One example of this is Galatians 3:28 where Paul states, "There is neither Jew nor Greek, there is neither bond nor free, there is neither male nor female; for ye are all one in Christ Jesus." This verse ensures that each woman has equal access to the Father's throne, and he loves and cares for us equally.

However, evangelical feminists insist "that in Christ, gender becomes irrelevant in shaping social roles and relationships." This view places the feminists and others in conflict with many New Testament passages which teach that Christians are to maintain gender-based roles (1 Cor. 11:1–16; Eph. 5:21–33; 1 Pet. 3:1; 1 Tim. 2:8–15; Titus 2). This conflict is handled in three ways.

First, some simply deny that the New Testament teaches a hierarchical model of male-female relationship. Face-to-face, others say that these teachings are no longer binding on twentieth-century Christians. A third approach is to say that Paul was in error because of inner conflicts caused by his rabbinical training.

Actually Galatians 3:28 says nothing about restructuring society.

- *In society there is still male and female.* Who is so sanctified as to want unisex restrooms?
- *In business there is still employer and employee.* Who would claim that a Christian employee should no longer obey his or her Christian boss?

- *In the home there is still parent and child.* Does salvation grant children immunity from obedience?
- *And in the church, though we are one in Christ, God still has his plan for church order.*

Again we should remember—equality of worth is not sameness of function.[3]

Some people do abuse the principle of headship in the home. Abuse of domineering husbands distorts the meaning of marriage. Those who deny the unique Christlike headship of the husband distort the meaning of marriage also. But how beautiful when a home operates under the principle of Kingdom Authority.

CHAPTER 12

IN THE CHURCH
LIFE

LEARNING TO FUNCTION AS THE BODY OF CHRIST

The grandest organization on earth is the church of our Lord Jesus Christ! Although it is an organization, it is not organized like a business. The church is organized as a body with Jesus Christ as its head—not as a corporation with Jesus Christ as its president. While Christ is the head, the saved are the members functioning under his authority.

First Corinthians 12:12–27 goes into great detail about this concept. Here are some excerpts from this passage on the church as the body of Christ:

> For as the body is one, and hath many members, and all the members of that one body, being many, are one body: so also is Christ. For by one Spirit are we all baptized into one body, whether we be Jews or Gentiles, whether we be bond or free; and have been all made to drink into one Spirit. For the body is not one member, but many. . . . And whether one member suffer, all the members suffer with it; or one member

be honoured, all the members rejoice with it. Now ye are the
body of Christ, and members in particular (vv. 12–14, 26–27).

The church operates just like our bodies, and whoever heard of a
body that is not organized? The body works together. It has organs that
function in relation to one another. That's what makes it a *body*.

I have heard some people foolishly say, "I don't believe in the organized church." I wonder what kind of church do they believe in—the *dis-
organized* church? Others have nonchalantly dismissed the church—
saying yes to Jesus but no to the church. That would be as foolish as
saying yes to the head and no to the body. This is what 1 Corinthians
12:21 is talking about, "And the eye cannot say unto the hand, I have no
need of thee: nor again the head to the feet, I have no need of you."
Indeed, that would spell disaster.

As the Head of His Church, Jesus Has Kingdom Authority Over It

"And Jesus came and spake unto them, saying, All power is given
unto me in heaven and in earth. Go ye therefore, and teach all nations,
baptizing them in the name of the Father, and of the Son, and of the
Holy Ghost: teaching them to observe all things whatsoever I have
commanded you: and, lo, I am with you alway, even unto the end of the
world. Amen" (Matt. 28:18–20).

The popular idea of the church being a democracy (the rule of the
people) is not found in the Bible. Nowhere does God tell us that
the church is a body "of the people, by the people, and for the people."
Indeed, there must be an expression of the will of God for the body.
This, as we will see, may show itself as a democratic process. But in spiritual reality, that process should operate under the headship of Jesus
Christ.

The church is a body "of the Lord, by the Lord, and for the Lord."
The body is to respond to, confirm to, and agree with what the sovereign
head is saying. The church always moves in a manner of response and

submission, not of self-willed initiation. It is a *Christocracy,* not a democracy.

The idea is not new. The concept of the church is seen when God created Eve from the side of Adam. She was made from Adam to be returned to Adam. In this way, Eve became a picture of the church. Just as Adam's bride came from him to be returned to him, all in Christ's church (the bride of the last Adam) must first emanate from him in order to be worthy to be returned to him. "For of him, and through him, and to him, are all things: to whom be glory for ever. Amen" (Rom. 11:36).

IN A BODY THERE IS TO BE A *MANIFESTED PERSON*

A body is a manifestation and expression of the person who lives in that body. The body itself is not the person but the manifestation of that person.

For example, everything that can be known about me can be deduced from my body. My revealed personhood is the sum total of what I say, write, and do. Of course, you can also learn about me by the way I look. You cannot see my spirit, but you can see my body. In the same way, we cannot see Jesus, but we can see him manifested in his body—the church. Jesus is the invisible part of his visible body (the church). Likewise, the body (church) is the visible part of the invisible Christ.

The church is his body, and he is to be expressing his life through the church. There is only one who has ever lived the Christian life—and that is Jesus. It will be lived anew and afresh when we let him manifest his person through his body the church.

IN A BODY THERE IS A *MINISTERING PURPOSE*

The body is to be the servant of the one who inhabits that body. Paul explains this by saying, "But I keep under my body, and bring it into subjection: lest that by any means, when I have preached to others, I myself should be a castaway" (1 Cor. 9:27). How does one "keep" his body? By submitting it to his head!

For a body to have plans of its own would be dangerous and bizarre. I would not want the five fingers of my hand to have a committee meeting, then determine that they are going to shave me, scratch my ear, or put anything in my mouth. The thought is frightening! The hand needs to be responsive to the head.

It will be a great day when we learn that Jesus does not want us to do anything for him. He wants to do *much through us.* We are the members of his body. Andrew Murray said, "Please note that this was what man was created for—to be a vessel into which God could pour His wisdom, goodness, beauty and power. That is the heritage of the believer. It is God that makes the seraphim and cherubim flames of fire. The unrestricted glory of God passes through them. They are vessels prepared by God, come from God, that they might let God's glory shine through them."[1]

The pastor's task is to help the members discover, develop, and deploy their gifts, and to let them serve at Jesus' command.

IN A BODY THERE IS A *MOTIVATING POWER*

The body is more than an organization. A corpse with every organ in place would be beautifully organized, but it would have no life. The body is an organism. Webster defines an organization as "an administrative structure." An organism, on the other hand, is defined as a "living thing."

The church can do nothing apart from the power—the Kingdom Authority power—of the Holy Spirit. Second Corinthians 4:6–7 illustrates this very well: "For God, who commanded the light to shine out of darkness, hath shined in our hearts, to give the light of the knowledge of the glory of God in the face of Jesus Christ. But we have this treasure in earthen vessels, that the excellency of the *power may be of God, and not of us.*"

The life of the human body is the human spirit, and the life of the church is the Holy Spirit. A body without a spirit is a corpse, and a spirit without a body is a ghost. Thank God, the church is neither.

In a Body There Is a *Mutual Program*

When a body is healthy, all the members have one agenda. It would be absurd to say, "The hand was so gifted that we sent it off on a mission on its own." A member of the body not under the authority of the head is in rebellion and causes difficulty for the other members of the body.

For example, if my ministry causes problems for your ministry, then I am wrong or you are wrong or we are both wrong. You see, we are all in the body of Christ, and each of us should function better because of the ministry of the other.

The problem is that we forget Jesus is the sovereign head of his church and he has mediated his Kingdom Authority *to* and *through* human leadership. This, by definition, means that there are to be under-shepherds in the church who have been given authority by our Lord to lead the sheep.

Sadly, in the modern church there is often a spirit of rebellion against human leadership. These people justify their actions because of a biblical doctrine called "the priesthood of the believer" which teaches the rights and responsibilities of all believers before God. This doctrine, though, does not negate God-appointed leadership in the church. The spirit of rugged individualism and autonomous selfhood is not to be the motivating power of a New Testament church.

Let me share what "the priesthood of the believer" does not mean.

1. *It does not mean that everyone's opinion is equally correct,* therefore, we all believe whatever we wish to be right. No! Not so long as there is truth and error. We must remember that there is basic content to the Christian faith. We should indeed live by our basic convictions, but basic conviction doesn't necessarily make those convictions right. The spirit of rugged individualism and autonomous selfhood is not to be an operating principle of a New Testament church.

When I was ordained to the gospel ministry, I was asked the same questions often asked by ordination councils. I had been forewarned about one question and was relishing the opportunity to answer it. "What would you do if the church refused to ordain you?" they asked.

Looking as much like a modern prophet as I could, I answered with firmness, "I would preach anyway."

This was my way of saying that it is God and not man who calls and ordains. That is truth. However, with age and experience, I think now I would give a different answer. Today, I might say something like this, "If you fail to recommend and the church fails to ordain, I think that I must reexamine what I perceive to be a call into the ministry. Please consult with me, instruct me, and pray with me more in this matter."

This is not to say that collective authority is final, but it is to say that we need to be careful about egocentric arrogance. Often pride and unbiblical independence keep us from submitting to those who have God-given authority.

2. *It does not mean, on the other hand, that the opinion of the majority is necessarily always right.* The truth of the matter is that the majority is almost always wrong. The majority doesn't come to prayer meeting, the majority are not soul-winners, and the majority do not live Spirit-filled lives. The majority in the church can have a party spirit. They can be manipulated, and they almost always favor the status quo.

3. *It does not mean that all in the church are basically the same.* All believers are of equal value and worth before the Almighty, but not all have the same gifts and corresponding spiritual authority in the church. There are God-given roles of ministry leadership and oversight (Acts 14:23, Titus 1:5, 1 Thess. 5:12–13, 1 Tim. 5:17, Heb. 13:7).

What "the priesthood of the believer" does mean is that each believer has direct access to God through the Lord Jesus Christ. He needs no human to practice priest craft in order for him to approach heaven's throne. The pastor is a priest for himself and no one else. He has no sacramental authority. Yet by his gifting, calling, and position, he is an undershepherd with spiritual authority in the church.

How then is a New Testament church to function as the body of Christ?

THE CHURCH IS TO BE PASTOR-LED

God gives divinely *appointed* and *anointed* pastors to lead his church: "Take heed therefore unto yourselves, and to all the flock, over the which the Holy Ghost hath made you overseers, to feed the church of God, which he hath purchased with his own blood" (Acts 20:28). The Holy Spirit of God is the one who makes the pastor the overseer.

A pastor is described by three basic terms in the New Testament. These are: elder (*presbuteros*), bishop (*episkopos*) and pastor (*poimēn*). These terms are found in Acts 20 and 1 Peter 5:12 in their noun or verb forms. They are different descriptions of the same office and ministry.

First, the pastor is an elder. This speaks of his *maturity*. In the Old Testament, elders were tribal leaders who assisted Moses in leadership. The word *elder* carries the idea of mature wisdom. It is not maturity that is measured by length of years but by spiritual growth. Timothy, who was young, was an elder, and Paul exhorted him: "Let no man despise thy youth; but be thou an example of the believers, in word, in conversation, in charity, in spirit, in faith, in purity" (1 Tim. 4:12).

Second, the pastor is a bishop, which speaks of his *management*. The Greek word literally means "overseer." This is the word picked up in the New Testament to designate the responsibility of a pastor or bishop. He is indeed an overseer. John MacArthur has this interesting insight:

> The bishops were those who were appointed by the emperors to govern captured or newly-founded city-states. The bishop was responsible to the emperor, but oversight was delegated to him. He functioned as a commission, regulating the affairs of the new colony or acquisition. *Episkopos,* therefore, suggested two ideas to the first century Greek mind: responsibility to a superior power, an introduction to a new order of things.[2]

Third, the pastor is a shepherd, which speaks of his *ministry*. The conventional meaning of this word is "shepherd." Like a shepherd, the pastor is to lead, feed, and protect his flock. And he is to lead, not by majority rule, but with God-given spiritual authority. Can you imagine a shepherd asking all of the sheep to vote on a particular pasture? The church therefore should look to pastoral leadership in the areas of godly maturity, gifted management, and loving ministry.

Several thoughts come to mind as part of this discussion on the roles of the pastor.

The first is that *the pastor is not a hireling.* The hireling flees. A good shepherd lays down his life for the sheep How foolish to speak of "hiring" a pastor. This conveys the idea that the minister is paid to do spiritual work on behalf of others. The truth of the matter is that he is to lead them and teach them to work. He is not a hireling. Warren Wiersbe said, "Ministry is too sacred to be motivated by gain and too difficult to be motivated by duty."

The membership gives its offerings to God, and in the last analysis it is God who pays the pastor. The pastor is there to lead the flock into ministry. For further study on this, I encourage you to read Ephesians 4.

Next, it needs to be stated that *the pastor is not a dictator.* I am often amused when people talk about dictatorial pastors. I believe there are few, if any, in Baptist churches. I serve at the pleasure of my congregation. The only leadership I have is what they *allow me to have.* They may dismiss me whenever they choose.

I heard of a pastor who subscribed to the theory of dictatorial leadership—but the congregation cancelled his subscription! Seriously though, no man, including a pastor, is free to pursue his own course within a local church. He is under the authority of the Word of God and the Spirit of God. Beyond that is the reserve authority of the entire body of the church. I find no justification for a pope over the whole church or for any individual church, for that matter.

However, it is not reasonable that a pastor should be given responsibility without corresponding authority. A pastor with authority is not a dictator. A dictator has authority with no accountability. A leader has responsibility and authority with accountability. The Bible makes clear that pastors must one day give an account of their responsibilities: "Obey them that have the rule over you, and submit yourselves: for they watch for your souls, as they that must give account, that they may do it with joy, and not with grief: for that is unprofitable for you" (Heb. 13:17).

Lastly, *the pastor's leadership is servant leadership.* The pastor is first a *servant* and then a *leader.* Any pastor not under authority has forfeited his right to exercise authority. Jesus is the sovereign Lord of the church, but notice his method of loving leadership.

> And he said unto them, The kings of the Gentiles exercise lordship over them; and they that exercise authority upon them are called benefactors. But ye shall not be so: but he that is greatest among you, let him be as the younger; and he *that is chief, as he that doth serve.* For whether is greater, he that sitteth at meat, or he that serveth? is not he that sitteth at meat? but I am among you as he that serveth (Luke 22:25–27).

This truth ought to make it clear that the pastor is not a boss or a dictator. God's sheep are not to be driven or herded but led by a loving shepherd. The apostle Peter understood this.

> The elders which are among you I exhort, who am also an elder, and a witness of the sufferings of Christ, and also a partaker of the glory that shall be revealed: Feed the flock of God which is among you, taking the oversight thereof, not by constraint, but willingly; not for filthy lucre, but of a ready mind; *neither as being lords over God's heritage,* but *being examples to the flock.* And when the chief Shepherd shall appear, ye shall receive a crown of glory that fadeth not away. Likewise, ye younger, submit yourselves unto the elder. Yea, all of you be subject one to another, and be clothed with humility: for God resisteth the proud, and giveth grace to the humble (1 Pet. 5:1–5).

Notice that Peter says, "I exhort," not "I order." Every pastor ought to aspire to the crown of glory that comes to a loving undershepherd. A word from Oswald Sanders is fitting here:

> The overriding need of the church, if it is to discharge its obligation to the rising generation, is for a leadership that is authoritative, spiritual and sacrificial. Authoritative, because people love to be led by one who knows where he is going and who inspires confidence. People follow, almost without question, the man who shows himself wise and strong, who adheres to what he believes. Spiritual, because a leadership that is unspiritual, that can be fully explained in terms of the natural, although eligible, attractive, and competent, will result only in sterility and moral and spiritual bankruptcy. Sacrificial, because modeled on the life of the One who gave Himself a sacrifice for the whole world, who left us an example that we should follow in His steps.[3]

What then is the proper response of a spirit-filled church to godly pastoral leadership?

One, we are to *remember, follow, and respect godly leadership:* "Remember them which have the rule over you, who have spoken unto you the word of God: whose faith follow, considering the end of their conversation . . . Salute all them that have the rule over you, and all the saints. They of Italy salute you" (Heb. 13:7,24).

Notice in these verses that there is a distinction between leaders and saints. All people in the church are equal before God, but all do not have equal responsibilities. All godly leaders are saints, but not all saints are leaders in the specific sense.

Next we are to *obey and submit to godly leadership:* "Obey them that have the rule over you, and submit yourselves: for they watch for your souls, as they that must give account, that they may do it with joy, and not with grief: for that is unprofitable for you" (Heb. 13:17).

According to the eminent Greek scholar A. T. Robertson, the word translated "obey" (*peithesthe*) is an imperative and means "to yield, to give up." This is not demeaning, nor does it harm. Let me illustrate. The traffic officer who works the school crossing for the children is a servant, yet he exercises authority. If he had no authority, his servanthood would be greatly impaired. Authority is given for the purpose of serving. Remember,

> submission is not subjection. Subjugation turns a person into a thing, destroys individuality, and removes all liberty. Submission makes a person become more what God wants him to be. It brings out individuality—it gives him the freedom to accomplish all that God has for his life and ministry. Subjugation is weakness; it is the refuge of those who are afraid of maturity. Submission is strength; it is the first step to true maturity and ministry.[4]

Your pastor has been given an awesome responsibility and needs your prayers. He is an overseer, a shepherd, and an elder. In my observation, the happiest and most fruitful churches are those that are blessed with strong, loving pastoral leadership.

And dear pastor, you must remember that you will never have the Kingdom Authority you should have if you fail to remain under the authority that God has put over you. Keep in mind, you are an undershepherd, and Jesus is your chief shepherd. When you have been called into the ministry, you are held to an even higher standard. Leadership is not only a privilege but also a responsibility.

THE CHURCH IS TO BE DEACON-SERVED

The word *deacon* (*diakonos*) means "servant" or "minister." Many times the word is used to describe anyone who serves (see Eph. 6:21). The word is also used in the official sense, describing those who hold the office of deacon (see Phil. 1:1).

Many believe that the office of deacon came into being at an event that took place in the life of the early church.

> And in those days, when the number of the disciples was multiplied, there arose a murmuring of the Grecians against the Hebrews, because their widows were neglected in the daily ministration. Then the twelve called the multitude of the disciples unto them, and said, It is not reason that we should leave the word of God, and serve tables. Wherefore, brethren, look ye out among you seven men of honest report, full of the Holy Ghost and wisdom, whom we may appoint over this business. But we will give ourselves continually to prayer, and to the ministry of the word.
>
> And the saying pleased the whole multitude: and they chose Stephen, a man full of faith and of the Holy Ghost, and Philip, and Prochorus, and Nicanor, and Timon, and Parmenas, and Nicolas a proselyte of Antioch: whom they set before the apostles: and when they had prayed, they laid their hands on them. And the word of God increased; and the number of the disciples multiplied in Jerusalem greatly; and a great company of the priests were obedient to the faith (Acts 6:1–7).

The early church was having growing pains. Growing pains are indeed a part of growing up emotionally and physically. It hurts to grow. Spiritually we can have growing pains also: "Hear me when I call, O God of my righteousness: thou hast enlarged me when I was in distress; have mercy upon me, and hear my prayer" (Ps. 4:1).

Churches can have growing pains and, as was true in the early church, it will be true in every church that grows.

WHERE THERE IS LIFE THERE IS GROWTH

God's command to the church is to "be fruitful, and multiply" (Gen. 1:28). And the early church was faithful to the call! In fact, the growth of the church was so dynamic that it was no longer addition but multiplication (Acts 6:1).

There is nothing wrong with a small church, but there may be something wrong with one that is not growing in spirituality and in numbers when they are in the midst of unsaved people. Numerical growth is the product of spiritual growth. We can grow and glow, or we can dry and die.

WHERE THERE IS GROWTH THERE ARE PROBLEMS

God wants to multiply us, and the devil wants to divide us. This was never more true than in the early church, which included two types of widows—Greeks and Hebrews. The Greek widows felt neglected. Remember that in this day there was no other resource of relief but the church for many of the widows' basic needs.

The problem was legitimate, but the method used to confront the problem was devilish and deadly murmuring. A murmur is a half-uttered and half-concealed complaint. It is the devil's way to divide when God wants to multiply. "Do all things without murmurings and disputings" (Phil. 2:14).

This problem was not doctrinal but functional. It was not primary but petty. There are always more opportunities for problems in a growing church. But I had much rather be in a growing church than a dead one.

WHERE THERE ARE PROBLEMS THERE ARE SOLUTIONS

The Twelve had a problem—who was going to serve the food and who was going to preach? (Acts 6:2–6). Led by the Lord, they discovered a very practical solution (the Bible is deeply spiritual but intensely practical).

God is a God of order. Disorder is a mark of carnality. God has commanded that all things are to be done decently and in order. It is the Holy Spirit that brought order out of chaos and made a cosmos in the creation story, and he will do the same in a church.

I am convinced there is no problem in churches too big to be solved, but there may be people too small to solve problems. It was clear there had to be the continued ministry of the Word of God (Acts 6:2, 4), and yet the church also needed people to help serve tables.

It was not that the apostles were too good or dignified to serve tables. God had given them a different assignment. Up until this time they had probably been serving tables but were getting behind with their prayer, sermon preparation, soul winning, and preaching. A wise man has said, "The pastor who is always available is not worth very much when he is available."

The plan was to choose some men to take care of this mundane but essential matter. There are a cluster of Greek words in this passage—variations of the word *diakoneō,* which means to serve.

The early church did not casually choose just anyone for the office of deacon. These were not inferior but superior men. It takes a superior man to serve. Jesus Himself came as a servant: "Even as the Son of man came not to be ministered unto, but to minister, and to give his life a ransom for many" (Matt. 20:28).

In Acts 6:3 we read the qualities that it takes to serve tables.

First, there is to be an established testimony of "honest report." A little boy saw deacons coming into the church, and he said, "Here come the beacons." Indeed they should be beacons of light. Leadership functions on the basis of confidence.

Second, he is to be full of the Holy Spirit. Nothing for Jesus can be done in the power of the flesh. Jesus said, "Verily, verily, I say unto you, The Son can do nothing of himself, but what he seeth the Father do: for what things soever he doeth, these also doeth the Son likewise" (John 5:19). If Jesus said he could do nothing apart from God, how can we say otherwise?

Third, he is to be full of wisdom. This means that it is better to have good men than smart men. Knowledge is important, but wisdom is paramount. Wisdom is the ability to use knowledge. What mighty men these were. Stephen was one of these men who preached one of the greatest sermons in the Scriptures. He became the first martyr. Another of these men, Phillip, was the layman, deacon, and evangelist who may have opened up all North Africa to the gospel. He was perhaps the first missionary.

These are the kind of men that a church should seek out for deacons.

WHERE THERE ARE SOLUTIONS THERE IS EVEN GREATER GROWTH

The problem referred to in Acts 6:4–6 was caused by growth, but when it was solved, the church grew even more. Problems are really opportunities in reverse. Thank God for your problems. Romans 8:28 says, "And we know that *all things work together for good* to them that love God, to them who are the called according to his purpose." Knowing this, you can truly thank God for all things. You never know, they may be the means of your growth when God is brought into the equation.

I love the deacons in our church. They are my personal friends and some of the most godly men I know anywhere. Many of our pastoral leaders have come out of our deacon body. Their bond is so evident that they do not call themselves a deacon board; they call themselves a deacon fellowship. When one thinks of a board, he may think of men sitting around a mahogany table making decisions for a corporation. These men, however, are godly, sensitive, winsome servants filled with wisdom and the Holy Spirit to free the pastor, not from work but to work.

I tell our deacons that there is no job that only a deacon may do and no job that a deacon may not do. They are to be available to serve. Service is not demeaning. Jesus taught that servanthood is the chief place of honor.

THE CHURCH IS TO BE COMMITTEE-OPERATED

The word *committee* is not found in the Bible, but the idea of commitment is. Remember, however, that there cannot be commitment to a cause without surrender to the Lord: "And the things that thou hast heard of me among many witnesses, the same commit thou to faithful men, who shall be able to teach others also" (2 Tim. 2:2).

If the church is analogous to a body, then a hand may be analogous to a committee. Through spiritual gifting God has affinity groups (a.k.a. committees) in the body that work together under the leadership of the pastor.

I'm not talking about committees leading a church. A "committee-led" church is disastrous. It would be very much a "hand-led" body. We have already talked about that.

Committees are made up of gifted people. In a New Testament church, it is so important that spiritual gifts be discerned, discovered, developed, and deployed. Spiritual gifts are tools, not toys. If you're in a Spirit-filled church, you will soon realize that you have been gifted by the Holy Spirit in areas of ministry and service. And as you grow in this knowledge and understanding of your gift, you can learn to cooperate with others in committees to get the work done.

In my estimation the modern church places too much emphasis upon "feel-good" religion and the church fulfilling "felt needs" for its members. I heard of a woman who gave a testimonial to her first-aid class that she was attending. She said, "There was a horrible automobile accident in front of my house. An old man driving his car hit an oak tree. He was thrown out of the car, and his skull was fractured. His eyes were rolling around in pools of blood. His bones were splintered. I thought I would faint, but I remembered my first aid. I remembered if I would put my head between my knees I would not faint."

I am afraid that's the kind of faith we are teaching today—faith that focuses on ministering to self instead of others.

We are called to serve. God has given us a commission to

Rescue the perishing, care for the dying,
Snatch them in pity from sin and the grave;
Weep o'er the erring one, lift up the fallen,
Tell them of Jesus, the mighty to save.

—Fanny J. Crosby

We are speaking about Kingdom Authority in the service of the King. And how is that done? Kingdom Authority is mediated in the church not only through gifted men—pastors that God gives to the church—but also through spiritual gifts that God gives to the members of the church. When anyone is gifted, he or she has a ministry; and whoever has a ministry has some authority. This does not mean that every member of the body of Christ has equal authority in every realm because of a spiritual gift.

The function of each member constitutes the authority. For example, the function of the eye is to see; the hand is to work; and the foot is to walk. We must learn to accept the function of other members. The function of the hand in the physical body is of great importance, but it has to accept the function of the feet when it comes to walking. The hand cannot feel color, so it needs to accept the authority of the eye when it comes to seeing.

Paul comments on this at length:

> And the eye cannot say unto the hand, I have no need of thee: nor again the head to the feet, I have no need of you. Nay, much more those members of the body, which seem to be more feeble, are necessary: and those members of the body, which we think to be less honourable, upon these we bestow more abundant honour; and our uncomely parts have more abundant comeliness. For our comely parts have no need: but God hath tempered the body together, having given more abundant honour to that part which lacked: that there should be no schism in the body; but that the members should have the same care one for another (1 Cor. 12:21–25).

We must remember, however, that while every member of the body has certain gifts and certain roles to exercise in the church, this does not mean that the church is to be operated as a pure democracy, but a theocracy. In a healthy church, the members learn to submit to one another.

A CHURCH IS TO BE CONGREGATIONALLY AFFIRMED

There is a wonderful spiritual ecology in a church that is operating in full Kingdom Authority. Remember, it is to be pastor-led, deacon-served, committee-operated, and congregationally affirmed.

The pastor, indeed, is to have a place of strong leadership, but he is not to be without accountability. The pastor and other church leaders still must submit to the reserve authority of the whole body because Jesus is the head of the body.

For example, if a pastor were to have a moral failure or fall into heresy, the congregation has the responsibility and the duty to bring that pastor to open rebuke: "Against an elder receive not an accusation, but before two or three witnesses. Them that sin rebuke before all, that others also may fear" (1 Tim. 5:19–20).

This should be done with the utmost care and in a spirit of holy fear. It would be extremely dangerous for a church to tolerate idle gossip or unfounded charges concerning its pastor. A pastor's reputation, based on his integrity, is his stock in trade. To hurt him in this area would be like cutting off an Olympic runner's legs.

Yet if there are grievous charges against the pastor that are proven, the matter should result in rebuke before the entire assembly. Sadly, in many churches the pastor is told to "get out of town" quickly so there will be no scandal. Then he slips away to some other unsuspecting congregation for a repeat performance.

The bottom line is this: a pastor is accountable to the congregation in which he serves. While a pastor is to lead, he is not a law unto himself. There is always the reserve authority of the entire body. The head cannot go where the body refuses to carry it.

A wise pastor will also realize his limitations and will consult with gifted members who will become partners with him in leadership. I have been kept from foolish mistakes many times by the wise counsel of dear friends in the church. I have also been given ideas and insights that I could never have come up with by myself. The pastor, indeed, may be the leader, but he is not all-knowing by virtue of the fact that he is a pastor. The humorist Will Rogers once said, "Everybody is ignorant, just on different subjects." How true that is. My leadership would be impoverished if it were not enriched by the incredible giftedness of the body.

When the first deacons were selected, the Spirit-led idea was introduced by the apostles, but it was affirmed by the body. The Twelve called the other disciples and said it was not reasonable for them to substitute their spiritual ministry for a physical ministry. They said they preferred to give themselves to pray, and with this the other agreed (Acts 6:2–6).

Woe be to any pastor who has such sense of his self-importance that he becomes authoritarian and fails to listen and to learn. Such an attitude shows immaturity and fear on his part. The true leader does not call honest questions and discussion "sowing discord."

The domineering leader has not learned to trust the Holy Spirit. A strong leader leads with honesty and openness. He will be loved and followed all the more. My plea is for there to be such a sense of love, leadership, and loyalty that a wonderful Kingdom Authority will be manifest in the church.

A. W. Tozer was a leader of another generation whose lament we should take seriously:

> The Lordship of Jesus Christ is not quite forgotten among Christians, but it has been mostly relegated to the hymnal, where all responsibility toward it may be comfortably discharged in a glow of pleasant religious emotion. Or if it is taught as a theory in the classroom, it is rarely applied to practical living. The idea that the Man Jesus Christ has absolute and final authority over the whole church and over all its members in every detail of their lives is simply not now accepted as true by the rank and file of Evangelical Christians.
>
> What we do is this: We accept the Christianity of our group as being identical with that of Christ and His apostles. The beliefs, the practices, the ethics, the activities of our group are equated with the Christianity of the New Testament. Whatever the group thinks or says or does is scriptural, no

questions asked. It is assumed that all our Lord expects of us is that we busy ourselves with the activities of the group. In so doing we are keeping the commandments of Christ.[5]

May it be said anew and afresh in every church—Jesus Christ is Lord!

CHAPTER 13

IN THE WAR LIFE

And they overcame him by the blood of the Lamb,
and by the word of their testimony;
and they loved not their lives unto the death.
—REVELATION 12:11

"They overcame him." These words speak of a battle and a victory over Satan. "But wait a minute!" someone says, "I thought Jesus had already overcome Satan. I thought the battle was over."

Here we need to learn the principle of appropriation. It is true that Satan has been defeated by bloody Calvary. He has been *stripped, shamed,* and *subdued* by the cross (see Col. 2:15). That is absolute in the legal sense (de jure), but it must be appropriated by the believer in a practical sense (de facto).

First, Christ's death for our sins is an accomplished fact, but it must be appropriated by faith. John 3:18 says, "He that believeth on him is not condemned: but he that believeth not is condemned already, because he hath not believed in the name of the only begotten Son of God." Because of Calvary people need not go to hell because of their sins. But they will go to hell if they do not by faith lay hold of the atonement.

Likewise, the Holy Spirit has been poured out on the church at Pentecost in all of his fullness and power. Yet many saints are living defeated lives because they have not appropriated the power of the Spirit. They have not possessed their possessions.

So we see the same truth in spiritual warfare. Satan's binding and the loosing of his captives must be appropriated by faith and prayer. Jesus has given us the victory, but we must lay hold of it. Jesus said, "Verily I say unto you, Whatsoever ye shall bind on earth shall be bound in heaven: and whatsoever ye shall loose on earth shall be loosed in heaven. Again I say unto you, That if two of you shall agree on earth as touching any thing that they shall ask, it shall be done for them of my Father which is in heaven" (Matt. 18:18–19).

This binding and loosing does not mean that God is saying, "I second the motion. I agree to bind what you bind and loose what you loose." Not at all!

The Greek tense shows that what we bind has *already been bound* in heaven and what we loose has *already been loosed* in heaven. We do not pray "upward" but "downward." The prayer that gets to heaven starts in heaven. We close the circuit. Prayer is the Holy Spirit finding a desire in the heart of the Father, and putting that desire into our hearts, then sending it back to heaven in the power of the cross.

Even the Lord Jesus Christ in his humanity did nothing in and of himself but looked to heaven and prayed from that perspective: "Then answered Jesus and said unto them, Verily, verily, I say unto you, The Son can do nothing of himself, but what he seeth the Father do: for what things soever he doeth, these also doeth the Son likewise" (John 5:19).

Is there a battle? Yes! Can we have victory? Absolutely! God has made this promise.

"We know that whosoever is born of God sinneth not; but he that is begotten of God keepeth himself, and that wicked one toucheth him not" (1 John 5:18).

We must depend on God; but when we "keep" ourselves, Satan cannot lay a hand upon us. We have been promised victory that is totally effective. "They overcame him," the Word declares. We are to be victors, not victims. We are to be overcomers—not to be overcome.

It is true that God for his sovereign purposes allows Satan to continue his warfare. There are people on earth who have chosen to listen to Satan's lies and live in his domain. That means that we as Christians at this time are living in hostile territory. Therefore, it does not mean that we will not know battles, but rather that we through spiritual warfare can know the ultimate victory.

Think with me a moment—we have been given authority over the world, the flesh, and the devil. But what does that mean?

Does authority over the world mean that I will have a place of prominence in the world's economy, rise to the top of my profession, that my football team will carry away the championship and that I will be honored by this world? No!

Does my authority over the flesh mean that I can now run faster, sleep less, and eat all I want? Does it mean that temptation will be a thing of the past? Of course not!

Does my victory over the devil mean that he can never oppose me or cause me physical hurt? Not at all. Think of what he has done to godly people in the past.

Paul, the mightiest missionary who ever lived, had an affliction (a thorn in the flesh), and he called it clearly "the messenger of Satan to buffet me, lest I should be exalted above measure" (2 Cor. 12:7b).

Simon Peter, the big fisherman, truly loved the Lord, but Satan sifted him as wheat (see Matt. 26). It is clear from the passage that God allowed it.

Stephen, whose face glowed like an angel as he was being stoned, was killed by an ungodly mob (see Acts 6). Yet who would say that Stephen was defeated by Satan?

What then is the authority over the world, the flesh, and the devil? It is that we do not have to give in to the world, the flesh, or the devil in the realm of temptation and sin. God's plan for us is not ease, wealth, or social status, but *holiness and victory.*

Indeed, God gives marvelous victories from time to time in the physical and material realms. God also works miracles in the material world. He often heals our bodies and dramatically delivers us from Satan's scheme. But we must remember that God is sovereign and makes these decisions in the council halls of eternity.

In Hebrews 11, we read about great victories and marvelous deliverances for the people of God; but we also read about some "others" who were not delivered.

> And others had trial of cruel mockings and scourgings, yea,
> moreover of bonds and imprisonment: they were stoned, they
> were sawn asunder, were tempted, were slain with the sword:
> they wandered about in sheepskins and goatskins; being desti-
> tute, afflicted, tormented; (of whom the world was not wor-
> thy:) they wandered in deserts, and in mountains, and in dens
> and caves of the earth. And these all, having obtained a good
> report through faith, received not the promise: God having
> provided some better thing for us, that they without us should
> not be made perfect (Heb. 11:36–40).

These did not *escape* by faith, but *endured* by faith. Yet they were also overcomers. Faith is not so much receiving from God what we want but accepting from God what he gives. It is one thing to have faith to escape; it is another to have faith to endure. Perhaps this enduring faith is the greater faith.

If I get sick, I am going to ask God to heal me. I believe that God heals by nature, by miracles, and by medicine. He heals naturally, and well as supernaturally. He heals instantaneously, and he heals in time. He *always* heals in eternity.

A prayer for healing is something like going to the bank president to ask for a loan. If the bank president believes that it is best for you *and* the bank, he may lend you the money. God may decide to "make me a loan" and heal my body. But I have no authority to claim it as I do when

I have money in the bank. In that case, I have the authority to sign a check and make a withdrawal.

When it comes to spiritual victory over the world, the flesh, and the devil, we already have authority. We can sign the check of faith and believe it will be done. We can be sure of that kind of victory because we have the spiritual cash in the bank.

Even in the realm of the physical, we are not at the mercy of Satan and his system. Anything that comes to us must go through the hands of God. God is never out of control. The holy Trinity never meets in emergency session. Not a blade of grass moves without the Father's permission. Satan had to get permission before he could torment Job. Satan had to get permission before he could sift Peter. Paul's thorn in the flesh was a messenger of Satan, but he said that messenger was given to him. It means that God was over it all.

How does our victory come? Look at this classic passage:

> And there was war in heaven: Michael and his angels fought against the dragon; and the dragon fought and his angels, and prevailed not; neither was their place found any more in heaven. And the great dragon was cast out, that old serpent, called the Devil, and Satan, which deceiveth the whole world: he was cast out into the earth, and his angels were cast out with him. And I heard a loud voice saying in heaven, Now is come salvation, and strength, and the kingdom of our God, and the power of his Christ: for the accuser of our brethren is cast down, which accused them before our God day and night. And they overcame him by the blood of the Lamb, and by the word of their testimony; and they loved not their lives unto the death. Therefore rejoice, ye heavens, and ye that dwell in them. Woe to the inhabiters of the earth and of the sea! for the devil is come down unto you, having great wrath, because he knoweth that he hath but a short time (Rev. 12:7–12).

From these verses, we learn that Satan is on his way down. The one who would have exalted his throne above the stars of God is on his way to the lowest hell. He was cast out of heaven and now continues the battle on earth. Yet that too is a losing battle for him because his doom is sure. Soon he will be cast into the lowest hell. He is a hopeless loser. Why would anyone follow him?

This passage reveals the three keys of victory against our ancient foe:

- the believer's conquest,
- the believer's confession, and
- the believer's courage.

THE BELIEVER'S CONQUEST

The blood of the Lamb speaks of the total victory that Jesus has already won for us at Calvary (Rev. 12:11). When Jesus was facing the cross, he declared, "Now is the judgment of this world: now shall the prince of this world be cast out" (John 12:31). He died for us, and therefore, we died with him. His death and victory was our victory.

THE BLOOD CONQUERS

At the cross Jesus devastated Satan's kingdom and brought it crashing down. Satan's back was broken by Calvary. Sin's debt was paid in full with Jesus' crimson blood. It is only a matter of time until this condemned felon, who has already been sentenced, is cast into prison. Hebrews 2:14 promises, "Forasmuch then as the children are partakers of flesh and blood, he also himself likewise took part of the same; that through death he might destroy him that had the power of death, that is, the devil." Through the blood of Jesus, Satan's power over us has been canceled, and we are set free.

Our primary passage in Revelation teaches that God is allowing Satan to continue for a "short time" in spite of the fact that his doom is sealed. He may be active, but he sails a sinking ship and rules a ruined domain.

After the Battle of Waterloo, Napoleon was in his war room with his generals. He had a map of the world on the wall and the British Isles were in red. He is said to have pointed at them and exclaimed, "If it were not for that red spot, I would have conquered the world." Surely, Satan must say that about Calvary.

THE BLOOD CLEANSES

What else does his blood mean to us? It means that we can be perfectly clean before God: "But if we walk in the light, as he is in the light, we have fellowship one with another, and the blood of Jesus Christ his Son cleanseth us from all sin" (1 John 1:7).

In spiritual warfare, it would be foolish to enter into battle without a clean heart. Unconfessed sin in the life of a Christian will not only nullify his victory but also make him vulnerable to Satan. Sin in the heart is like an enemy behind the lines. It is a devastatingly crippling power.

The apostle Paul warned against such unconfessed and uncleansed sin: "Be ye angry, and sin not: let not the sun go down upon your wrath: neither give place to the devil" (Eph. 4:26–27). These verses teach us the danger of letting simmering anger (or any sin for that matter) abide in our hearts. It is giving Satan a beachhead, a campground in the life. The one who has given Satan such a place can resist, rebuke Satan, or whatever he wishes, but Satan will not budge until that unholy ground is taken back by confession and cleansing through the blood.

Is it any wonder that so many believers are being tormented, obsessed, and defeated? They have given to Satan an unholy campground inside the ranks of their personality.

James also gives clear directions about spiritual warfare. "But he giveth more grace. Wherefore he saith, God resisteth the proud, but giveth grace unto the humble. Submit yourselves therefore to God. Resist the devil, and he will flee from you" (James 4:6–7). The order is always this—first we submit to God and then resist the devil. To try to resist Satan with pride in the heart would be no more effective than arguing with Niagra Falls in the hopes of stopping the water. The truth is that not only will Satan not be resisted; Almighty God himself resists the proud person.

But the good news is that because of the blood of Jesus there is no reason that any Christian should not be absolutely clean when he can confess and be cleansed. "If we confess our sins, he is faithful and just to forgive us our sins, and to cleanse us from all unrighteousness" (1 John 1:9). How foolish to be other than perfectly clean. Satan fears a holy Christian.

THE BLOOD GIVES ACCESS

"Having therefore, brethren, boldness to enter into the holiest by the blood of Jesus . . ." (Heb. 10:19). As a believer, I can now come into the inner sanctum of heaven with my prayers because of the blood.

The biblical temple was an object lesson of this spiritual truth. In that temple was a sacred spot called the holy of holies. God's shekinah glory dwelt there. It was a forbidden place for anyone to enter except the high priest, who could enter there only once a year. The high priest would go behind the veil that separated that holy inner sanctum with a basin of blood to sprinkle upon that piece of furniture called the mercy seat. There atonement was made for the sins of Israel. All of this, however, was temporary and symbolic. It pictured and prophesied what Jesus would do in reality in the future.

When Jesus died, the old system was fulfilled and became defunct. The veil that closed off that inner sanctum was torn by the hand of God from top to bottom. It symbolized that the humblest saint could now enter into the true holy of holies—heaven—by the blood.

What does this have to do with spiritual warfare? Much! The battle will be won or lost in prayer. Satan knows this. Satan mocks at our intentions, sneers at our schemes, and ridicules our organizations but fears our prayers. I can imagine one demon saying to another as he looks at our lives. "Whatever you do, keep them from praying. If they pray, they will be victorious every time. If we can keep them from praying, they will live in defeat." Satan cannot keep God from answering, so he tries to keep us from asking. Thank God that we can come boldly to the throne because of the blood.

In the blood we have victory, cleansing, and access. What mighty weapons these are for overcoming the enemy.

THE BELIEVER'S CONFESSION

The second key to victory in spiritual warfare is the word of your testimony (Rev. 12:11). What does this mean? Is your testimony simply describing the day of your salvation or letting others know how much Jesus means to you? It may include those things, but it goes far beyond them.

The word of our testimony centers also in Jesus. It is an open declaration of his mighty victory. See how the apostle John speaks of this testimony in the Book of Revelation.

> Who bare record of the word of God, and of *the testimony of Jesus Christ,* and of all things that he saw (Rev. 1:2).
>
> I John, who also am your brother, and companion in tribulation, and in the kingdom and patience of Jesus Christ, was in the isle that is called Patmos, for the word of God, and for *the testimony of Jesus Christ* (Rev. 1:9).
>
> And the dragon was wroth with the woman, and went to make war with the remnant of her seed, which keep the commandments of God, and have *the testimony of Jesus Christ* (Rev. 12:17).
>
> And I fell at his feet to worship him. And he said unto me, See thou do it not: I am thy fellowservant, and of thy brethren that have the testimony of Jesus: worship God: for *the testimony of Jesus* is the spirit of prophecy (Rev. 19:10).

All of these verses on testimonies speak of Jesus—who he is and what he has done. It speaks of his ultimate victory.

Therefore, in our spiritual warfare we must use the word of our testimony. We need not only to believe the power of the blood, but we need to speak it with no uncertain terms. We need to speak of the victory of Jesus on our behalf in our relationship with him.

Testify Who Jesus Is

The way to victory is the word of our testimony concerning Jesus. Testify about his glory, rejoice in his victories, and meditate on his names. Praise him constantly. Satan is allergic to and defeated by such praise.

Read Revelation 12:11 in its context. It is a wondrous story. A Lamb has defeated the great dragon! The Lamb has prevailed! All glory to the Lamb! The word of our testimony is Jesus' glorious victory over Satan.

Testify Who You Are

The word of your testimony also includes you because you are in Christ. You have been co-crucified, co-buried, co-risen, and co-enthroned with Jesus. His death, burial, resurrection, and ascension were on your behalf and had your name on them.

A part of the word of your testimony is to see yourself and to speak of yourself as an overcomer. This is important because *the me I see is the me I'll be.* We often hear God's people speak of themselves with what they imagine to be humility. "I know I am not much. I know I am no good. I know I am just a sinner saved by grace."

Well, technically you may be just a sinner saved by grace, but the Bible doesn't call you that. The Bible calls you the righteousness of God in Christ (see 2 Cor. 5:21).

We need to see ourselves as God sees us—*kings and priests.* We need to see ourselves with Kingdom Authority. We were made to reign in life. By our new birth we were brought into the family of God. God is our Father, and Jesus Christ is our elder brother. We can consider ourselves to be a prince or a princess. We are royal bluebloods.

Remember, it is Satan who is accusing us night and day (see Rev. 12:10). What fools we are if we agree with him and cooperate with him.

Listen to what Paul said about Satan's accusations: "Who shall lay any thing to the charge of God's elect? It is God that justifieth. Who is he that condemneth? It is Christ that died, yea rather, that is risen again, who is even at the right hand of God, who also maketh intercession for us" (Rom. 8:33–34).

The word of your testimony is to see yourself as God sees you—redeemed, accepted, empowered, and given Kingdom Authority. This is not to say that we should be flippant about our sins and fail to confess them. Yet we need to see who we are in the Lord Jesus Christ.

You can say to yourself, "I am a child of God. I am Christ's friend. I am chosen and appointed by my Lord. I am a son or daughter of God. I am a member of Jesus' body. I am an heir of God. I am a saint. I am God's workmanship. I am chosen by God, holy and dearly beloved. I am a member of a chosen race, a royal priesthood, a holy nation; and I am what I am by the grace of God."

TESTIFY WHO SATAN IS

Revelation 12:9 tells that Satan is an outcast and a deceiver. His kingdom is ruined, and now he operates only by a system of lies (John 8:44).

Satan will bluster and intimidate. He will come as a roaring lion or an angel of light. Yet we should not be terrified or enticed. I am not saying that we should trivialize Satan. Martin Luther said, "His power and craft are great and armed with cruel hate, on earth is not his equal."

Yet greater is he who is in us (Jesus) than he who is in the world (Satan). All of this is a part of the word of our testimony.

Satan's power is limited. Some have wrongly supposed that Satan could snatch a Christian from the hand of Jesus. How foolish! Think for a moment. If Satan could snatch you away from Jesus, why hasn't he? Is it because he is being good to you? That would be a strange doctrine, would it not? You would be going to heaven by the goodness of the devil! No! The only reason Satan hasn't snatched you is because he can't (see John 10:27–29).

Another word is in order here. We hear much about demon possession. The King James Version of the Scriptures often uses the phrase "possessed with devils" in passages like Matthew 4:24; 8:16, 28, 33; 9:32;

12:22. The same wording is found in many other versions. The Greek term means to "have a demon." No one is under the total control of Satan at all times. In the most severe case of the man whose name was Legion because he possessed so many demons (see Mark 5), there was still enough freedom for that poor man to run to Jesus and fall on his knees. A man totally possessed would not be able to do that.

Don't give Satan more power than he has. Have you ever played the game of antonyms? I say one word and you give the opposite. I say *good,* you say *bad.* I say *up,* you say *down.* I say *light,* you say *dark.* I say *God,* you say *Satan.* No! Satan is not God's opposite. God has no opposite. Satan is a creature under the control of Almighty God. Don't give him greater status than he has. All of this is a part of the word of our testimony. It tells us that the weakest believer, the smallest child has victory because of the indwelling Spirit who lives in us.

An uneducated man was reading the Book of Revelation. A scoffer said, "You can't understand that book. Why are you reading it?"

"Oh, but I do understand it," said the joyful saint.

"Well, then explain it to me," the scoffer said.

"OK, I will be glad to explain it to you. *We win!*"

I want to say *amen* to that. The ultimate victory of Jesus is the word of our testimony.

So what is the word of your testimony? It is an open, bold, and clear confession of your victory. Remember that Jesus is the high priest of your testimony (Heb. 3:1). Give your high priest words of victory to present to the Father in heaven. This is not a "name it and claim it" theology. It is laying hold of what God has promised and what God has named. Since our Lord has proclaimed it, we can profess it and claim it joyfully. "He hath said . . . So that we may boldly say . . ." (Heb. 13:5–6).

This is important in our prayer life. We need to pray in keeping with the word of our testimony. As I have suggested earlier, here are some ways to encourage your faith:

- Rather than "Lord, be with us," pray, "Father, we welcome your presence."

- Rather than "Lord, give us victory," pray, "Lord, you are our victory. I thank you to cause us always to triumph."
- Rather than "Lord, defeat Satan," pray, "Lord, I thank you that Satan has been defeated by your shed blood."
- Rather than "Lord, give me strength," pray, "Lord, you are my strength, shield, and deliverer."
- Rather than "Lord, help me to be a better servant," pray, "Lord, I consciously yield myself to you. I report to duty."

And remember to speak aloud the word of your testimony. What good is a testimony if it is not declared? When Satan comes against you, resist him with the word of your testimony. I want to make it clear that we don't pray to Satan but we do resist him. Don't bargain with him, don't argue with him, and there is no need to shout at him. When you are aware of his activity, you can lift your head and speak like this: "Satan, you are a liar. Jesus is Lord, and he has defeated you at Calvary. My life belongs to him. My sins are all under his blood. My body is the temple of the Holy Spirit. I refuse your lies. You have no right or authority in my life. There is no unclean spot where you have any right to dwell. You are trespassing on my Father's property. In the name of Jesus, I refuse you and resist your power in my life."

Jesus rebuked Satan openly and verbally (Matt. 16:23). Just as Jesus rebuked Satan verbally, so may we. We are not praying to the devil anymore than we are praying to a cat when we say "scat."

Satan is like a hobo. He has no rights that we do not give him. We can demand that he leave. After he has gone, we may have to clean up the trash.

But whenever we resist Satan in this fashion, he may still be allowed to hinder and afflict the saints in many ways. This is a part of the mystery of iniquity. I want to be very clear that it does not mean that Satan has won or is winning the victory. This becomes clear in the third key of victory.

THE BELIEVER'S COURAGE

Verse 11 of Revelation 12 also speaks of Christians who are willing to die for their faith. It does not mean simply that they live for Jesus until they die. It means that they will be true to him even if it costs their lives. And Satan has been behind the massacre of many Christians.

The newspaper carried an interesting story. The heading said, "Dead Rattlesnakes Are Still Deadly." A portion of the article said:

> Doctors in Arizona have a warning for the public: a rattlesnake can bite you, even if its head has been cut off . . . one patient was bitten when he picked up a snake he had bludgeoned with a piece of wood until it stopped moving. Another man was bitten when he picked up a snake three minutes after he had shot it several times in the head. Two men were bitten when they picked up heads they had chopped off . . . previously, research has shown that snakes' reflexes remain functional after they are dead, allowing them to bite for as long as sixty minutes after decapitation.

Satan, the old serpent, is much like that. He has been mortally wounded at Calvary, but he still has lethal power. It is true that he must operate under the limits that God sets for him. Earlier we mentioned saints who have suffered at the hand of Satan but only because God allowed it for his sovereign purpose.

In spiritual warfare can we get hurt? Yes, but we can't ultimately be harmed. This sounds like a contradiction, but it is not. Jesus told of persecution that would come to the saints (Luke 21:16–18). Notice the contrast in this remarkable passage. He speaks of those who would be put to death, and yet he says, "Not an hair of your head [will] perish." We almost feel like saying, "Well make up your mind; which will it be?" The truth is, in the ultimate sense Satan cannot harm even one hair!

All that Satan does ultimately backfires on him. God will get the glory no matter what. The Scripture teaches that God makes even the wrath of man to praise him.

My Romanian friend, Joseph T'son, was being harassed by the Communist thugs in Romania. This was the time under the brutal dictatorship of Ceausescu. He was warned, "Joseph, if you don't get in line and register with the Communist government and let us control your ministry, you know what we can do to you." Joseph answered, "I know what you can do. Your chief weapon is killing, but let me tell you what my chief weapon is. My chief weapon is dying. And I want to warn you, if you use yours, I will be forced to use mine."

When Joseph was asked what he meant by using dying as a weapon he said, "If you kill me, you will sprinkle every book that I have written, every sermon that I have preached, with my blood. People will know that I believed enough in what I preach to die for it. So if you use your weapon, I will be forced to use mine."

The Communist enforcer shook his head and went away bewildered.

We have recently seen what some would call a tragedy on our American soil. Cassie Bernall lived in Littleton, Colorado. She was a seventeen-year-old junior with long blond hair, hair that she wanted to have cut off and made into wigs for cancer parents who had lost their hair through chemotherapy. She was active in her youth group at West Pool's Community Church and was known to carry a Bible to school. She had had a profound experience with Christ and wrote this note:

> Now I have given up everything else. . . . I have found it to
> be the only way to know Christ and experience the mighty
> power that brought Him to life again, and to find out what it
> really means to suffer and die with Him. So, whatever it takes,
> I will be one to live in the fresh newness of life of those who
> are alive from the dead.

She was in the Columbine High School library when a gun was pointed at her face. She was asked, "Do you believe in God?" She took a deep breath and answered with a clear voice "Yes!" "Why?" the gunman asked. Before she could answer, the trigger was pulled, and this young martyr was face-to-face with Jesus Christ. It seems hardly doubtful that Satan inspired the two students who shot thirteen people. Yet the whole matter has backfired on Satan. Multiplied millions have heard the saving gospel of Jesus Christ through this young martyr's death, and God alone knows the number of those who have put their faith in him as a result.

The age of martyrs is not over. More than one hundred million people have been killed for the Christian faith in this century alone. It is so true that the church is "watered by the blood of the martyrs." Not only do we overcome by the blood of the Lamb but also with our own blood.

Another gripping story illustrates this truth. A gunman opened fire inside the Wedgewood Baptist Church in Fort Worth, Texas, on September 15, 1999. He killed seven people and injured seven others before taking his own life. That morning had been the day of "See You at the Pole" when students gathered around the flagpole in the morning to pray for their school and nation. Satan may have been infuriated and caused the attack, but look at what has happened.

Because of the live news coverage and interviews, over two hundred million people have heard the gospel. Here is a report from a member of the church:

> Fifteen thousand turned out for a community-wide service at the TCU football stadium. The service was broadcast live on a news station that covers most of North Texas. CNN also broadcast the memorial service. Amazingly, because one of the victim's families lives and works in Saudi Arabia, that country allowed the service to be broadcast there as well. In Saudi Arabia it is illegal to say the name of Jesus on the street.
>
> It is reported that because of the same CNN broadcast thirty-five people in Japan gave their lives to Christ. At several schools, students met around the flagpoles the next day. At one school twenty-five students accepted Christ. One hundred and ten did the same at another school. A teacher led twenty-two

students to Christ in her classroom as they discussed the event.

The church's Web site has been inundated by people wanting information. The church is giving out the plan of salvation in multiple languages.

What an illustration of God's Word. "Be sober, be vigilant; because your adversary the devil, as a roaring lion, walketh about, seeking whom he may devour: Whom resist stedfast in the faith, knowing that the same afflictions are accomplished in your brethren that are in the world. But the God of all grace, who hath called us unto his eternal glory by Christ Jesus, after that ye have suffered a while, make you perfect, stablish, strengthen, settle you" (1 Pet. 5:8–10).

Indeed, where Satan rules, God overrules. Sometimes our chief weapon may be dying, but remember the words of Jesus: "Not a hair of your head shall perish."

> I saw the martyr at the stake,
> The flames could not his courage shake,
> Nor death his soul appall.
> I asked whence his strength was given.
> He looked triumphantly to heaven
> And answered, "Christ is all."

EPILOGUE

One more time, let me ask the question . . . What is Kingdom Authority? It is the right delegated and given to us by God to act for him in spiritual matters.

Charles Kraft has called it the "Jesus Credit Card" in a book entitled, *I Give You Authority,* in which he uses this slice-of-life illustration:

> "Dad, would you put your name on my VISA card? I am going off to college 1500 miles away, and the car may break down. You wouldn't want me to be stranded somewhere without being able to pay the bill would you? I promise that I won't misuse it."
>
> These words were those of my son, Rick. They all made sense to me, though I was a bit apprehensive about whether he would keep his word or not and misuse the card. But he is my son, my own flesh and blood, and I was an important part of his latest adventure. I knew that, in addition to paying his tuition, my granting him this request made sense. My name would still appear first on the card as the one with the ultimate responsibility. But Rick's name would appear immediately under it, giving him authority to spend whatever the company would allow me by way of credit.
>
> When my son's name was added to my credit card he gained all of the financial authority that my name would bring. At that time my son's name carried no authority since he had no credit with any financial institution. But with my name to back him, he would be able to handle almost any emergency that might confront him far from home.

When I did this for my son I made it clear that I expected him not to misuse the authority that I was giving him. He was young and might have well misused it, and he needed to keep on good terms with me or his privilege might be revoked. But to his credit he never misused the privilege.[1]

I think that is a great illustration of spiritual authority. With that in mind, what must our relationship be to Kingdom Authority?

WE MUST NOT REFUSE KINGDOM AUTHORITY

While Kingdom Authority is inherently ours through the cross, we may willfully or ignorantly refuse to exercise it. How tragic if you fail to appropriate your authority. You will give Satan a free hand to run roughshod over you and those who are meant to be under your protection. How can we refuse to take authority over Satan when those under our care are being harmed?

Suppose your home is being robbed or your children are being assaulted. You call the police, and they come to your house and stand and watch the harm being done. Perhaps they make small talk and sing songs about their authority while your loved ones are suffering. They refuse to use their delegated authority. How ridiculous this would be!

Likewise, how sad when we refuse to exercise our God-given authority. Pastors must protect their flock, parents must protect their family, and leaders must protect those under them against the one who comes "to steal, and to kill, and to destroy" (John 10:10). A father should serve notice to Satan: "If you want to get at my wife and family, you will have to come through me, and I will not allow that."

WE MUST NOT CONFUSE KINGDOM AUTHORITY

Remember that all authority is delegated. God forbid that the husband should somehow think that his authority emanates from himself and thus become lord over his house rather than the protector and servant. The man must remember that in himself he is of no more value than the weakest member of the family.

Another confusion comes when some people feel that with authority they can command or coerce God or Satan by using certain phrases like "in the name of Jesus" or "I claim the blood" or "I command it to be done." This may be akin to magic or superstition rather than spiritual authority.

Of course, there is power in the name of Jesus and His precious blood, but they cannot be used like a sorcerer trying to cast a spell. These should not be confused with submission and obedience to the Father in the true exercise of authority.

We Must Not Misuse Kingdom Authority

It is sad to see Kingdom Authority misused or abused for selfish purposes. How sad for anyone to attempt to use spiritual authority in a way that it was not meant to be used.

We are stewards. We must use our authority for the purpose it has been entrusted to us. First Corinthians 4:2 says, "Moreover it is required in stewards, that a man be found faithful."

The pastor has been given a place of authority, but he must be careful to stay on his face before God and not misuse the authority over the flock that God has entrusted to him. Of course, the same should be said for every person in authority in whatever realm.

We Must Not Abuse Kingdom Authority

We abuse Kingdom Authority when we attempt to command God to do our will. Authority is not a means to get earth's will done in heaven. Rather, it is a means to pursue heaven's will performed on earth.

We abuse Kingdom Authority when we make our plans, then expect God to ratify and rubber-stamp them.

We abuse Kingdom Authority when we act in arrogance, pride, and presumption. Authority is not a license to do as we wish or to desire what we want. It is also not a "name it and claim it" magic wand that we wave in front of a holy God.

We abuse Kingdom Authority when we order the world to believe us because of our delegated authority, then fail to serve in love.

WE MUST USE KINGDOM AUTHORITY

I have tried to share my heart in this book. Certainly, there is much more that I need to learn about Kingdom Authority. I know that this volume is not the final word, and I will be the first to confess that I need to put into practice more and more of the things that I have tried to teach.

But I do know this—ours is a needy world. I know that Jesus in all of his grace and power is sufficient to meet every need. I also know that he has redeemed and empowered the church with Kingdom Authority. He has given his mandate for world evangelization: "And Jesus came and spake unto them, saying, All power is given unto me in heaven and in earth. Go ye therefore, and teach all nations, baptizing them in the name of the Father, and of the Son, and of the Holy Ghost: teaching them to observe all things whatsoever I have commanded you: and, lo, I am with you alway, even unto the end of the world. Amen" (Matt. 28:18–20).

WE HAVE HIS UNLIMITED POWER

The word *power* in the Great Commission means "authority." Jesus is Lord with no rival and there can be no rebuttal.

He has power in heaven (the heavenlies). This speaks of the spirit realm of principalities and powers. It speaks of his dominion over angels and demons. He also has authority on earth. His is a worldwide domain. There is no place he does not belong and no power that he cannot break. Because of this there is no person he cannot use.

WE HAVE HIS UNCHANGING PROGRAM

We are here to make disciples of all nations. Anything less is unworthy of our Lord. The modern church is often guilty of giving first-class efforts to second-class causes. As a result the church is defeated by secondary successes.

I saw an amazing picture in the newspaper. A grown woman had her ear on the chest of a grown man. The man was not a relative of this woman's, but he had received a heart transplant from the woman's son. She was listening to the heartbeat of her own son. Would to God that he could put his ear upon our chest and hear the heartbeat of his Son, which is world evangelization.

WE HAVE HIS UNFAILING PROMISE

His presence is with us; his authority is behind us; his commission is before us. With all of this assurance, we ought to adopt the motto of the French Foreign Legion:

> If I falter, push me on.
> If I stumble, pick me up.
> If I retreat, shoot me.

Think of it—what a promise! *All* authority, *all* nations, *all* commandments, *always.*

Most of us do not dare dream what God will do with us, through us, and in us. But this can change if we say from our hearts that Jesus Christ is Lord and begin to live like it. To God be the glory!

NOTES

Chapter 3, Taking Back Lost Ground

1. Francis Schaeffer, *A Christian Manifesto* (Westchester, Ill.: Crossway Books, 1981), 28.

Chapter 6, Limits of Our Kingdom Authority

1. Barbara Lee Johnson, *Count It All Joy* (Grand Rapids: Baker Book House, 1978), 31.

Chapter 7, The Problem of Unworthy Authorities

1. Carl M. White, *Light,* The Ethics & Religious Liberty Commission of the Southern Baptist Convention (March-April, 1999), 4.

2. Francis Schaeffer, *A Christian Manifesto* (Westchester, Ill.: Good News Publishing/Crossway Books, 1982), 90.

Chapter 9, The Authority of the Word of God

1. John Murray, "The Attestation of Scripture," in *The Infallible Word: A Symposium,* by members of the faculty of Westminster Seminary (Philadelphia, Pa.: Presbyterian and Reformed Publishing Company, 1946), 4–5.

Chapter 11, In the Home Life

1. Wayne Grudem, "Wives like Sarah, and the Husbands Who Honor Them: 1 Peter 3:1–7," in *Recovering Biblical Manhood and Womanhood: A Response to Evangelical Feminism,* ed. by John Piper and Wayne Grudem (Wheaton, Ill.: Crossway Books, 1991) 194–205.

2. Ibid.

3. Joyce Rogers, "Women Ministering Under Authority."

Chapter 12, In the Church Life

1. Andrew Murray, *The Believer's Absolute Surrender* (Minneapolis, Minn.: Bethany House Publishers, 1985), 45.

2. John MacArthur Jr., *The MacArthur New Testament Commentary: Ephesians* (Chicago: Moody Press, 1986), 145.

3. Oswald Sanders, *Spiritual Leadership.* (Grand Rapids: Discovery House, 1999).

4. *Leadership,* winter 1980, 82.

5. A. W. Tozer, *The Waning Authority of Christ in the Churches,* (Camp Hill, Pa.: Christian Publications, 1995).

Epilogue

1. Charles H. Kraft, *I Give You Authority* (Grand Rapids, Mich.: Chosen Books, 1997), 34.